FROM
LUCIFER
TO
LAZARUS

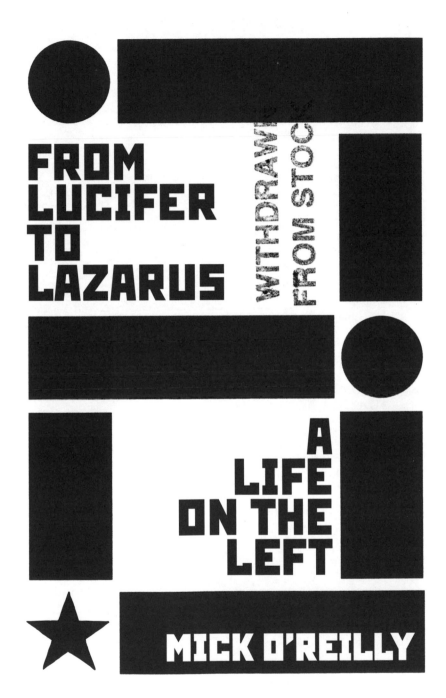

FROM LUCIFER TO LAZARUS

WITHDRAWN FROM STOCK

A LIFE ON THE LEFT

MICK O'REILLY

THE LILLIPUT PRESS
DUBLIN

First published 2019 by
THE LILLIPUT PRESS
62–63 Sitric Road, Arbour Hill
Dublin 7, Ireland
www.lilliputpress.ie

Paperback ISBN 978 1 84351 764 1
Ebook ISBN 978 1 84351 775 7

A CIP record for this title is available from
The British Library.

10 9 8 7 6 5 4 3 2 1

The Lilliput Press gratefully acknowledges
the financial support of the Arts Council/
An Chomhairle Ealaíon.

Set in 11.5 on 17pt Garamond by Marsha Swan
Printed by Drukarnia Skelniarz, Poland

CONTENTS

Illustrations   vi

Abbreviations   viii

Foreword *by Len McCluskey*   ix

Introduction *by Gene Kerrigan*   xi

Prologue   xv

ONE 1

TWO 8

THREE 18

FOUR 27

FIVE 37

SIX 45

SEVEN 53

EIGHT 61

NINE 70

TEN 77

ELEVEN 87

TWELVE 100

THIRTEEN 111

FOURTEEN 121

FIFTEEN 131

SIXTEEN 142

SEVENTEEN 159

Acknowledgments   171

Appendix 1   173

Appendix 2   175

Index   189

ILLUSTRATIONS

Illustrations between pages 110 and 111.

Mick O'Reilly aged six, at home in Ballyfermot, Dublin, 1955 (photo: Anna Ashmore, eldest sister).

Mick and his sister Anna on O'Connell Bridge, Dublin, 1958 (photo: Arthur Fields, *Man on the Bridge*).

Mother, Lucy (*née* Watts), with Anna and Mick, aged twelve, at his sister Teresa O'Reilly's wedding in Birmingham, 1958.

Mary (*née* Brien) and Mick O'Reilly on their wedding day, Inchicore, Dublin, 1972.

Meeting of the Connolly Youth Movement (CYM) at the Irish Workers' Party HQ, Dublin, c.1968.

Flyer advertising the forming of a branch of the CYM in Sligo, 1968. Chairman Declan Bree later became a Labour TD and independent socialist councillor.

Protest against entry to the Common Market, 1972.

O'Reilly speaking at a recruitment rally for the Communist Party on Abbey Street in Dublin, 1973.

O'Reilly at a conference on Marxism with Sam Nolan, Joe Deasy, Bernard Browne and Eamon Dillon, at the ATGWU office on Abbey Street in Dublin, 1984.

Protest against the downgrading of services at Louth County Hospital, Dundalk, 1989.

The Irish Times: Brendan Byrne (SIPTU) and Mick O'Reilly (ATGWU) at the Labour Relations Commission after receiving news of the closure of the Packard plant in Dublin, 1995 (photo: Peter Thursfield).

Amalgamated News: The Amalgamated Support Group campaigns for the restoration of Mick O'Reilly and Eugene McGlone to office following their dismissal, 2002.

Amalgamated News: Mick O'Reilly and Eugene McGlone thank supporters following the announcement of their reinstatement, 2003.

O'Reilly with Eugene McGlone, Deputy Regional Secretary of the ATGWU, Belfast, 2005.

O'Reilly with the late Joe Deasy, the last living councillor who served with Jim Larkin, 2007.

O'Reilly seated with Jack McKay, David Ervine, William 'Plum' Smith, Billy Hutchinson; standing up, Maurice Cunningham, Norman Cairns, Davie McMurray, Eugene McGlone, Alison Gribben, Billy McCracken and John Curran in discussion with the Progressive Unionist Party in the Transport House, Belfast, 2008.

O'Reilly with lifelong friend Bernard Browne at a social function in the Dublin ATGWU office, 2011.

O'Reilly commemorating the 1913 Lockout with Jack O'Connor, Eoghan Runane, Jimmy Kelly, Ger O'Laoghaire and others outside Leinster House, Dublin, 2013.

Mick O'Reilly, Declan Bree and Liam Mulready at a CYM celebration in Wynn's Hotel, Dublin, 2014.

Mick O'Reilly today, 2019.

Recruiting poster by Conor McHale, addressed to archaeologists, 2014.

Mocked-up cover for *From Lucifer to Lazarus* by Conor McHale, 2019.

ABBREVIATIONS

AEU	Amalgamated Engineering Union
ATGWU	Amalgamated Transport and General Workers' Union
CP	Communist Party
CPNI	Communist Party of Northern Ireland
CWC	Catholic Workers' College
CYM	Connolly Youth Movement
DHAC	Dublin Housing Action Committee
ESB	Electricity Supply Board
ETU	Electrical Trades Union
IBEC	Irish Business and Employers' Confederation
ICTU	Irish Congress of Trade Unions
IDATU	Irish Distributive and Administrative Trade Union
ILDA	Irish Locomotive Drivers' Association
IRSP	Irish Republican Socialist Party
ISME	Irish Small and Medium Enterprises Association
ITGWU	Irish Transport and General Workers' Union
IWP	Irish Workers' Party
NBRU	National Bus and Rail Union
NUVB	National Union of Vehicle Builders
SIPTU	Scientific, Industrial, Professional and Technical Union
SLP	Socialist Labour Party
TD	Teachta Dála
TEEU	Technical Engineering and Electrical Union
TGWU	Transport and General Workers' Union
TSB	Trustee Savings Bank
TUC	Trades Union Congress
WUI	Workers' Union of Ireland
YCL	Young Communist League

Foreword

My own life as a trade unionist and activist began on the Liverpool docks, so one incident in Mick O'Reilly's memoir struck a particular chord with me.

During the protracted and bitter Liverpool docks dispute of the 1990s, Mick O'Reilly, as Irish Regional Secretary of the ATGWU, not only arranged collections for the dockers but also assisted them when they travelled to Drogheda to try and stop a boat being loaded for Liverpool. Apparently the Liverpool lads slept on the floor of the ATGWU Drogheda office before travelling up to Dublin the next morning. I have a feeling, however, that they may have been sampling the Guinness rather than sleeping!

It was a small incident in an action-packed memoir, but typical of the man and his life: the principle of solidarity has guided Mick as a worker and activist, as a union official, and today in retirement.

From Lucifer to Lazarus charts a Dublin working class life, from the O'Reillys' move to Ballyfermot from an inner city tenement, via Mick's political activism to his role as a trade union official and, finally, head of the T&G in Ireland – a position from which he was dismissed in controversial circumstances only, like Lazarus, to be reinstated following a bitter battle spanning two jurisdictions.

This memoir brings late twentieth-century Ireland to life – socially, industrially and politically. Mick O'Reilly not only witnessed, but actively participated in, many of the events and campaigns that formed modern

Ireland, including the Dublin Housing Action Committee and the 1983 debate around the Eighth Amendment.

As a member at different times of both the Communist Party and the Labour Party, O'Reilly is ideally placed to dissect the fractious relationship between different elements of the Irish Left, and does so with gusto. While never electorally strong, the Irish Communist Party exercised a disproportionate intellectual influence on Irish trade unionism and Left politics and Mick provides a unique insider's perspective on the workings of the Party, including the bitter debates on the Soviet Union's invasion of Czechoslovakia which both Mick and the Party condemned.

Mick writes as he speaks. This memoir shines a pithy, acerbic and occasionally erudite light on the development of the Irish trade union movement and the Irish Left. Along the way, he offers illuminating pen portraits of friends and foes alike.

The thread running through *From Lucifer to Lazarus* is an unswerving belief in the power of people to organize collectively – and the power of the resulting collective action. That belief has informed Mick's 'Life on the Left', and indeed my own life. It is at the heart of what we, as trade unionists, are about.

Len McCluskey
General Secretary
Unite the Union

Introduction

In June 2001 RTÉ's *Morning Ireland* informed the nation that the Regional Secretary of the ATGWU, Mick O'Reilly, had been suspended. Also removed from office was Regional Organizer Eugene McGlone. This, the news programme reported, was due to an 'extensive administrative audit' of O'Reilly's stewardship of the union.

The *Morning Ireland* report was based on a story in *The Irish Times*. The reporter who wrote the story was interviewed and asked what kind of audit was involved. Was it about 'how things are run, or how money is spent, or both?'

'It's everything,' explained the reporter. 'It's finance, it's how things are run ...'

I remember breathing a weary sigh. The suspensions took place during a period in which various sorts of corruption in public life were coming to light. It wasn't a surprise that a scandal had emerged in a trade union. The unions, like everything else, are run by humans, and none of us is immune to temptation.

But if anyone could resist putting his fingers in the till, I thought it would have been Mick O'Reilly. I didn't know him personally (since then I've met him once, briefly) but I knew his reputation as an implacable class warrior, totally committed to the trade union movement. In a society that too often values people not by what they do but by what they accumulate,

O'Reilly was one of those who seemed to have higher values. To use the old phrase – he did not seek to rise above his class, he sought to rise with his class. He supported his own members in their fight for better pay and conditions. Beyond that, his principles and instinct led him to support anyone fighting for a fairer world. The Labour movement is full of such people, banding together in self-interest, committed to a wider solidarity.

Still, lefties are as vulnerable as anyone else to the laws of temptation. So, bugger it, I concluded. There was no escaping the fact that one of the good guys had been caught doing what he shouldn't. It was the word 'audit' that did it. You don't 'audit' someone's work rate or their competence, you measure it. You audit finances. It was obvious that this wasn't about O'Reilly becoming lazy or careless on the job. Much as I didn't like the idea, the conclusion had to be that if the union was doing an audit, it was because union money had gone missing or had been in some way misused.

I write for the *Sunday Independent*, and had written about various scandals. As it happened, I knew some people in the union, people fiercely protective of the integrity of the movement. Such people might respect O'Reilly's record, but they wouldn't stand for any betrayal of the union. As an outsider, I expected them to refuse to badmouth O'Reilly, or at best, be lukewarm in defending him. Instead, they quietly, and in convincing detail, explained the background to the 'scandal' and confirmed their trust in him. There was no issue of financial wrongdoing. O'Reilly's militancy hadn't gone down too well in certain quarters, words were quietly spoken, an 'audit' was arranged, and inevitably word got to the media. O'Reilly's memoir explains how the alleged scandal fell apart over the next two years.

In a few words, on a radio programme with more listeners than any other in the country, O'Reilly's well-deserved reputation for honesty and decency had been destroyed. I can't think of another occasion in which a reputation was so thoroughly shredded in so few words. The media was doing its job, reporting in good faith on a public development, so there was no libel involved. It wouldn't have been as damaging had it been a vicious tabloid attack rather than a sober report by a radio programme with a solid reputation.

Mick O'Reilly's memoir shows us what it's like to be at the centre of such a devastating thrashing, and how he and Eugene fought back. His story goes beyond that, portraying a life lived in a culture and a class that rarely gets media space, and from a radical and unapologetic point of view.

Had certain cuddly trade union leaders, politicians, journalists or academics been attacked as O'Reilly and McGlone were – had they had their reputations and their careers smashed, been gagged, forbidden to speak about what was being done to them – and had they somehow got the message out, there would have been widespread outrage. Are we not, they would have asked, a democracy? The answer is: yes, we are – for some. For others, defined by class, race or gender, not so much. Which is why both O'Reilly and McGlone, and their trade union comrades who supported them, knew immediately what was happening, and why.

Gene Kerrigan

Prologue

'Who steals my purse steals trash; 'tis something, nothing;
'twas mine, 'tis his, and has been slave to thousands;
But he that filches from me my good name
Robs me of that which not enriches him,
And makes me poor indeed.'
William Shakespeare, *Othello*

On 25 June 2001 I flew back from holiday in Lanzarote, landing in Dublin around 3.30 am. My phone had been stolen while I was away, so I was out of communication. I drove home and had a terrible night's sleep.

The following morning, 26 June, I put four sugars in my coffee to wake myself up – and I don't usually take sugar. RTÉ's industrial correspondent Peter Cluskey came out to record an interview with me at 9 am on the appointment of David Begg as the new General Secretary of the Irish Congress of Trade Unions (ICTU). It was a ten-minute interview to be put in the can in time for the ICTU conference the following week.

As soon as that was done, I had to drive to Belfast for a meeting in the office of the Amalgamated Transport and General Workers' Union (ATGWU). On the way I picked up Ben Kearney in Finglas, who was also going to the meeting. We had a great chat. He was my deputy in the union and was just about to retire, and I was saying that we could get him to do some part-time work for us, that I would nominate him to the employment appeals tribunal – in brief, that I would find a role for him. Retirement is a big deal in a person's life. It was a very amicable, engaging conversation. I asked him what would come up at the meeting and he said, 'Ah, nothing much, just a bit of moaning over the train drivers, but what's new?' That was it. I had no idea he'd been in contact with London.

We arrived in Belfast. Present at the meeting in Transport House were Jimmy Kelly and Norman Cairns, members of the ATGWU executive, the chair of the Irish region Jackie McCoy, the vice chair Alex Thompson, Eugene McGlone the regional organizer, myself and Ben Kearney. People asked how my holiday had gone.

Eugene McGlone said, 'I'm after getting a phone call from Lillian Deery in the Derry office. Harry McBride [Harry was on the regional committee] has said that we're going to be suspended this morning – that we're going to be gassed.'

'Fuck off out of that, Eugene, and don't be annoying me with scare stories,' I replied.

'I'm telling you!' he said emphatically.

I looked out of the window and saw Jimmy Elsby, who had been Scottish regional secretary and recently promoted to a job in London and wasn't supposed to be at this meeting. I saw Sharon Withers – a peculiar person to be there because she was the financial administrator in the union. And I saw Ray Collins, the eyes and ears of the General Secretary who had worked in the union since he was in the boy scouts, a competent and able apparatchik who knew everything and believed nothing. I became a bit apprehensive.

'I told you so,' said Eugene.

We were about to start the meeting – with just a normal trade union agenda – when Collins leaned over to me. 'Can I see you privately in your office? I have a letter for you from the General Secretary.'

I said it would wait until after the meeting, but he insisted. We went next door into my office. He handed me a letter and said he wasn't sure what was in it, then proceeded to tell me as I tore open the envelope and read the letter. I was flabbergasted. It said that matters had come to Bill Morris's attention and I was under precautionary suspension. I had to leave immediately. I was not to communicate with anyone in the union, or enter a union office. I could keep my mobile phone and my car. They'd let me know if they found anything once the investigation was over.

I'm not easily alarmed, but the effect was the same as having a sawn-off shotgun pointed at my head. I was dumbstruck, clueless as to how to proceed. Yet despite the shock, two things struck me. The letter mentioned 'a number of matters that have been brought to my attention', which sounded like he didn't have a case yet but was going to shake the trees until he found one. Then I'd been told not to talk to anyone in the union, 'nor any third parties with whom the union deals'.

'I have a meeting with our members in the TSB tomorrow,' I said to Collins.

'Well, you'll just have to not have it.'

It hit me that this union was prepared to leave people behind while they made wider decisions. I was out. The enormity of what was happening began to sink in.

Collins told me not to talk to anyone and the first words that came out of my mouth were, 'Are you telling me I can't go to mass because the Catholic Church is an institution the union deals with? Can I not talk to my wife Mary? She's a member of the union.'

'The words mean what they mean. You should leave the office now.'

I might have hit him, had I stayed, caught between being dumbfounded and angry. As I was leaving the office, my secretary, Valerie Cornish, said, 'Oh, Mick, the staff will all walk out!'

'Valerie, I'll probably never be back here again. Don't put yourself at risk,' I replied. She was close to retirement and persisted in saying she would leave. In the end I got her to stay.

I walked out the front door of Transport House and hadn't gone three steps down when I stopped. My whole life was crashing down around me.

What should I do? I have to fight this union but I don't know how to, or if I can.

A feeling of utter bewilderment surged through me. Of course you do things wrong in a union. Something happens every day; you're in conflict with people, arguing and taking decisions, signing off on expenses. But I couldn't think of what I might have done. In time I began to realize that I had to go the fifteen rounds, but on that morning in June 2001, I no longer knew where I was, or who I was.

ONE

The powerlessness of kindness, of senseless kindness, is the secret of its immortality. It can never be conquered.

Vasily Grossmann

Cork Street in the early 1950s was a special place for smells. They assaulted the senses. The decaying meat from Keeffe's, overlaid with the hops from the Guinness brewery, which hung over the whole of the Liberties, and then the reek of Jeyes Fluid, permeated every room and corridor. I have vague memories of the tenement I grew up in, but I can't be sure whether the stories have just been told so often that they've become reality. I do remember Morelli's, the fish and chip shop next door, and crawling under the tables there, and the darkness of the tenement.

Our bedroom was downstairs, at the back of the building. I never saw the rats but I know they were there. My father, a gunsmith, took home a torch and a pellet gun to kill them. I remember us three kids lying on the bed with the torch watching as he did in the rats. That was pure enjoyment for us; there was no question of poverty or awfulness. In fact, we were probably better off than a lot of people. There would have been five of us children had my mother not lost two boys before me who all died shortly after being born. She then underwent a medical procedure and I was born in the Coombe hospital on 21 October 1946. The painful reality of working-class life is that although I lost my brothers, we had more money.

My father was a builders' labourer before the war. He was working where the family lived, in Crumlin, paying a flat rather than a differential rent. Differential rent was something you might expect in an advanced left-wing state – you were allocated a house on the basis of your social need and paid for it according to your ability. Essentially, the policy followed Marx's principle and came from Jim Larkin's time on the Corporation, influenced by what was going on in other countries. (It was unpopular with some workers because the income they got from overtime was included when the rent was calculated.)

When my father lost his job we could no longer afford the flat rent so we moved back to the tenement. It must have been a huge setback for my mother to have to move from a Corporation house back into a tenement. The houses in Crumlin were built by a Corporation direct labour scheme, where you worked three months on and three months off. Just before the Second World War started in 1939 my father went to England to work on an aerodrome. My mother told me he won the fare to England in a coin-tossing game in Crumlin. It sounds harrowing, but it was seen as a normal thing to do.

My father ended up joining the army. He had previously been a boy soldier, having joined the British army in Dublin at the age of fourteen soon after the First World War and using his elder brother's name and age to enlist. He served in India for a good few years and learned how to make curry, which was extremely exotic in Ballyfermot back then. He served in the artillery in the Second World War, and was on the ack-ack guns in Dover, then developed a heart condition and subsequently received a pension from the British army, an extra bit of a cushion against the normal poverty.

After the war he worked for my mother's brothers as a gunsmith and specialized in adjusting individual gun stocks. It was an unusual profession, but every job has its perks: ours was plenty of fish and fowl, because some of his wealthier clients would bring him a perch or a pheasant or whatever. He'd take me clay pigeon shooting, and fishing. But I have very little memory of my father because he died so young: he developed angina and was dead at the age of fifty-two, when I was only seven and a half.

We moved out to Ballyfermot in 1949 or 1950 to a corner house with a big garden, the last house on Landen Road, number 453. There was a great sense of freedom in being able to just run around the garden. The other thing I couldn't get over after we moved out of the tenement was that our new house was both upstairs and downstairs. We had a neighbour in Cork Street, Mr Fogarty, who'd lost a leg in the First World War and who my sisters used to help on the stairs. I remember saying in Ballyfermot, 'Is Mr Fogarty upstairs?' I just couldn't get used to the idea. The way they built in Ballyfermot was amazing: they started at the top of the road, but the bus only went to the bottom. Landen Road is nearly a mile long, and we'd have to walk over a building site to get the bus.

I remember when my father died. He was leaning down to put the lead on our dog for my sister and I to take it for a walk, and just fell down. There was no one else in the house, and we didn't know what to do. We had no phone at home – the nearest one was at the top of Kylemore Road. My sister ran up there and called the doctor, but my father was already dead by the time he got to us. My mother later said to my sister, 'Oh, you should have got his tablets and put one under his tongue.' It was only a casual remark, but fifty years later my sister told me how much it still weighs on her.

My mother's pension from the British army was a bit more than the widow's pension she would have got, so we weren't the poorest family in Ballyfermot, but it was tough enough. I don't remember hunger. You had to be careful with the food, of course, and there was no waste, but at the time there was very little choice. My mother used to shop in Fay's in Meath Street, which had everything. You'd see rabbits hanging up and you'd pick one, and there was bacon and butter and tea. There was just butter; not a million different types of butter, just butter. There were only two types of bread. Biscuits were just broken biscuits in a bag. There was tea, just one type of tea. The quality of the food was good. People couldn't afford lots of it, but it was nearer to where it came from, and vegetables were in season. Food was very regimented, a day for this and a day for that, and it never varied. If you were lucky you had meat on a Sunday, which might carry over for a day or two, a stew one day, a fry another day. Most households were the same.

There was no political tradition in the family. My father would have voted for Clann na Poblachta and a lot of people in working-class areas did, because they thought they offered a kind of alternative. Sometimes there would be arguments. I remember a sharp conversation between my parents when it was announced on the BBC Home Service that Stalin had died. My mother thought it was a good thing, that religious freedom would come back in the Soviet Union. My father didn't disagree with that, but like a lot of people he had a sneaking admiration for Stalin, having survived the Second World War as he did. What must it have been like hearing the news that thousands of German soldiers had surrendered to the Red Army at Stalingrad and that the war was effectively won?

During a butchers' strike and a picket on the butcher on Decies Road, my mother made a remark that's come back to me over the years: 'They're fighting for their bread.' I was bemused by butchers fighting for bread, and it was only years later that I understood that 'bread' has a wider meaning. Lots of revolutions have been fought over the price of bread. I later worked in Johnston Mooney & O'Brien and was in the Bakers' Union for a short period, and I remember the union lobbying for an increase in the price of bread so that we could get an increase in our wages, all the while looking up and down the street to make sure none of the other union members saw us!

I was enthralled by my first Communion, and went through the motions with huge levels of sincerity and commitment. Catholicism has a lot of collective values, and the idea of all these children dedicating themselves to a wider Church has a particular appeal. I still regard myself as culturally a Catholic even though I haven't been in a church to worship since I was about twelve years old. It's part of my being, what I was reared with. The smell of incense still takes me back to childhood.

The whole family went shopping the day before my Communion and my mother bought me a very nice second-hand blue suit and a fawn Crombie coat in Francis Street market. It didn't get any better than a Crombie in Ballyfermot. We then went to Johnny Ray's ice-cream parlour in Francis Street, where my sister was delighted to be given three wafers with her ice cream instead of the usual two.

The next day I was walking down Decies Road to the school with my friend from next door. I remember my coat kindling a feeling of division between us and it didn't feel right, so I walked down to the corner – the turn into Thomond Road – took the coat off and bundled it under a hedge. He said nothing, but there was a sort of smile and I felt at one with him. So I carried on down to the school, happy as a pig in shit, until I spotted my mother on the street. All I can say is I'm glad I found that coat again. I couldn't explain myself to her, didn't want her to feel that somehow she'd done something wrong, but I resented the fact that she didn't understand.

Inequality is more than just a concept: it's instinctive. I read the terrific *Life and Fate* by Vasily Grossmann, in which he talks about the danger of big ideas, Stalinism, fascism, the Gulag, the Holocaust, and that what really matters is small acts of 'senseless kindness'. Humans – particularly children – have an instinctive feeling for freedom and tolerance. It's part of the human spirit and we should aim to achieve a society where as little of it as possible is lost. The socialist movement is in danger of losing it with its many silly intolerances and bragging about sectarianism towards one another. I've tried to avoid sectarianism during my life. People in the Communist Party used to tell me not to work with Trots, and Trotskyists would tell me not to work with Stalinists.

We were always going to the pictures when I was a kid, as often as four times a week. The Gala cinema in Ballyfermot was one of the biggest in

Ireland, perhaps even in Europe, holding nearly two thousand people. I went the first week it opened to see a black-and-white film called *Blowing Wild*, with Gary Cooper and Barbara Stanwyck. Before the Gala we would regularly go to the Tivoli or the Phoenix.

My sister Teresa is four years older than me, and Anna, the eldest, is eleven years older. It was a very warm household. As the baby of the family, I was let away with everything, and I suppose there was an extra bit of affection for me because the other three boys died. The downside was a lack of discipline. My sisters went to school in town: they took the bus from Ballyfermot to Whitefriars Street school and Weavers Square school but my mother didn't like the idea of me going in on the bus. In 1954, when I was six and a half years old, I started in the De La Salle school in Ballyfermot. Then, when my father died, I missed school for two or three months because I was very ill. I was eleven, just into fifth class, when I left for good. My parents probably weren't tough enough with me to make me go, and so I ended up with no formal education.

The Brothers were very violent. Although I never experienced it myself apart from a couple of slaps, I saw them kneeing and using leathers and canes. They attempted to teach us through fear. Education has gone through a complete transformation since, and I marvel at my own children and grandchildren and how they love going to school. It wasn't all bad: you were with your mates, getting up to things, keeping busy, and I did learn how to read and write, just about – and that's a powerful thing. As Brecht said, 'Hungry person, read a book: it's a weapon.' That's always stuck with me, and I've always read a lot. But it was a cram shop, an absolute cram shop. I've a photograph with over fifty kids in the class. How do you teach fifty kids? Of course religious people in Ireland gave a lot to education, but certainly the Brothers were violent towards the kids.

I didn't like sport. We'd drill in Croke Park before big matches, dressed in white with the school emblem in green. A band played, and you moved to their tempo. It was like the mass parades in fascist countries or in the Soviet Union. But I fell well behind after my father died. The rest of the boys were drilling every week, but I had been out for several months after his death and couldn't keep up with the movements. A few of us who kept getting it wrong were pulled out of the crowd to stand and wait. One of the head Brothers, Brother Leo, came up and twisted my ear – not terribly hard, he just twisted it – but I had an abscess in my ear canal at the time and the pain of it was excruciating. In my agony I headbutted him; he fell backwards and I scarpered over the wall, in front of the whole school. I didn't really go back to school after that. It was near the holidays anyway and I might have gone back for a while after, but then I just left for good.

TWO

We've been accused of a lot, but I wouldn't like to add kidnapping to it.

Johnny Nolan

I did very little after I left school. There was talk of going to the technical school, but in 1960, around the time of the massacre of Irish UN troops in the Congo, I answered an ad in the paper and got a job in Howard's of Capel Street as a presser, making women's clothes for thirty-eight shillings a week, ironing the inside seams so they would be flat for the linings. There were about a hundred women there, but the three pressing jobs were done by men, two older lads on the machines and me doing the seams by hand. It was a payment-by-results system, so I had to be fast to keep up with the women. It was good but hard work.

Although I should have handed my keep to my mother, I didn't. I finally had money to buy books, and I also started drinking – usually cider in the fields, graduating to pints in the pub. I was fourteen or fifteen when

I was first served in a pub, in Mattie Langan's. Of course there was a strong drinking culture later on in the socialist and trade union movements: no meeting was complete without a pint afterwards, where the real meetings took place and the real decisions were made.

I worked in Howard's for just over a year, until one day there was a bus strike. My sister, who worked in May Roberts, a chemist on Grand Canal Street, had always given me lifts home on her scooter but never lifts to work since we started at different times. But the boss insisted I work overtime. I said I couldn't or I'd lose my lift and so he sacked me. That was my first experience of employers and their power. I could have come in earlier, but there was no discussion, no compromise. It was, 'I have the power and you do as I say, or you don't do it here.' I had no redress – the union wasn't strong, and I wasn't even in the union. I vowed never to be in that situation again. And although I had many scraps with employers, I never had to fight for myself again. Still, what he did was completely unreasonable and still rankles with me today.

Then I got a job in a place called Stirling's, near Suir Road Bridge, sorting scrap metal – lead here, copper there – and putting it into barrels. That union was better organized, but there was no shop steward. I then moved on to May Roberts, where my sister also worked. The committee in the Irish Transport and General Workers' Union was called the drugs committee – there was even a drugs branch! The shop steward was Robbie Kavanagh, quite an ethical sort of man, very conservative. His brother became auxiliary bishop of Dublin and wrote a book called *A Manual of Social Ethics*, which Paddy Carmody dissected month by month on the back page of *The Irish Socialist*. Robbie was a decent man, but weak, totally reliant on the idea that if you explained yourself to your betters, they would somehow find a way of looking after you.

We did overnight runs, and country runs where you came back the same day and for which you got dinner money and tea money. One of the van drivers was Jim Devves, and I occasionally went with him. The total allowance was two shillings and sixpence, but he'd give me six penny Gifty toffees instead of the six pennies, keeping the rest. I rebelled. It's interesting that the first row I had on the job was not with the company but with another worker. Within the working class, the distribution of resources is not always fair – but it was dealt with, and he handed over the money. He was just chancing his arm but it was child labour, really. I worked six days a week, including a half-day on Saturday, so two and sixpence was a lot of money, and taking two shillings out of it was a big deal.

One of my pals, Bernard Browne – he's still one of my best mates – was sacked along with another person for playing cards on the job. The chemists would put in the order and you went to the shelves and put it in the box. They'd work away, putting away the orders and playing a card here, turning a card there – but was it damaging the quality of the work? These people had families, yet they were just sacked with no warning.

And the workforce was passive. The rationalizations were like scenes from *The Ragged Trousered Philanthropists*: 'Well, sure, what else could you do? The employer had no choice.' I was appalled. I went to the union but didn't even get a hearing.

Bernard got another job. I also left and walked into a completely different world, a car assembly plant making British Leyland cars called Lincoln & Nolan down in Wapping Street on the quays. There must have been five or six hundred people working there. I started at 1.30 pm on 21 October 1962, my sixteenth birthday. A foreman, Tom Dent, interviewed me for the job. He asked me a couple of questions, told me I'd be working in the stores, and then – this hadn't happened to me in any other job – said, 'Go and see the shop steward.'

I went to see the shop steward, Billy Wheatley. At that time in the factory there was a small group of people who used to say the rosary at lunchtime and Wheatley said: 'Them fuckers are up there praying for overtime. But kid, you don't mind them. You join the union, and we'll get you time and a half for it. That's the way this place operates.' That went into my lather of thoughts. There's something different about this place. Billy really looked after me and the conditions were fantastic: I worked a 35-hour week because I was under eighteen, but got paid £4 17s for forty hours, a huge increase compared to May Roberts.

The whole atmosphere was different. It wasn't madly left wing, but the attitude to management was, 'If you want us to do something, ask us. And you'd better listen to us, because we have a point of view on things.' We had rows, bans on overtime, meetings in the canteen. When I went to my first union meeting in Lincoln & Nolan, I was absolutely amazed at these fellas I worked with, wearing their Sunday suit, being able to articulate about the cost of living. Everyone was as good as the people at the top table. People in the union had been to Britain, bringing a slightly more left-wing stance. The National Union of Vehicle Builders was a very militant union with a different structure, and in the British unions there was more of an emphasis on rank-and-file involvement.

A lot of unions today don't want to let go like that. A good union is one that does things for you, but it must also teach you to do things for yourself. There is often a lack of self-belief in the working class, that they can't get involved in negotiations or take responsibility, that they need a 'professional' to do it for them. That leads to consumer trade unionism, where you pay an official to work magic for you. The various union bureaucracies are not all the same. A leader in the Transport and General Workers' Union in Britain is a very different animal to a leader of SIPTU here.

Nowadays in the trade union movement no one on the Right ever gets elected. They may end up being on the Right, but when they're running for election in a union now, everybody's left wing, more left wing than each other. When I was first active in the trade union movement, there was a contestation between Left and Right, with the Left being smeared generally with communism. There was a feeling that people in the Communist Party might be working for another state. Ordinary fellas would have a reservation about you in the back of their mind: they might elect you to be the General Secretary of the union, but they'd never elect you to be prime minister of the country. Éamonn McCann tells a story about his father, who was a daily communicant but always voted for communists in union elections. He said the communists were the best people to look after you on earth, and the Church would look after you afterwards. Working-class people had that pragmatic attitude.

When I first joined the union, one of their campaigns was to spread out production over the whole year. This was before the Redundancy Payments Act: people would be laid off for a few months and then taken back, and others would be weeded out. The union had a campaign to create continuity of employment, requiring the employers to carry a stock of fully built-up cars to balance them over the year in order to make roughly the same amount all the time. We forced the employers to carry the extra costs of balancing production to meet our human needs. That's a valuable lesson. It wasn't a Left–Right argument, because everyone agreed that this was what we should do. They kept at it and won.

It's important for trade unions to have ambition beyond simply wages and conditions. James Connolly, in his 'syndicalist' phase, talks about trade unionists being soldiers who are going to move into this area of control. Wresting control and influence from employers isn't an absolute, except in some kind of final revolution, but consists of acquiring bits and pieces of power. Gramsci is perhaps the greatest socialist writer on the idea of workers being organized as producers. Before Leninism there was a theory that socialism was about the freedom of producers. When you deal with productivity, output and efficiency, there has to be something in it for you.

The participation in and understanding of wealth production as part of the trade union agenda is critically important. The struggle between labour and capital is not just about wages, but about what and how you produce; and what we managed to do later, in the 1970s, was to erode the prerogatives of management and their control of production. That's an important ambition for unions to have and nurture.

Billy Wheatley was helpful and encouraging, a shop steward as well as an active member of the Labour Party. He was the first person to tell me, when I was sixteen or seventeen, that I should look to lead the union one day. 'I've never met anyone so young that had such potential,' he once said. I had no idea what he was talking about.

Billy was a great wit. He worked in the underbody section of the production line with Jimmy Ronan, who we called 'Jimmy Ronan, the Mother of Sorrows'. Jimmy was about four foot six, and Billy was about six foot four. Obviously, if you're working in the underbody, it's better to be four foot six. We made three basic bread-and-butter cars: the Mini, the A40 and the A60, but maybe once a year we'd make a Princess, or a batch of four of them. They would wait to get four orders, and they came in CKD (complete knock-down) packs to be broken down and assembled. The chat was that one of these Princesses was for President Éamon de Valera. Whether it was or not I'll never know, but some of the fellas wanted to add two coats of paint and extra bitumen because it was for de Valera, while others were against it. The company made it clear that it was to be treated just like any other Princess.

Wheatley was in the underbody, pushing up the sump of the car when a big crack appeared. This was a disaster: ordering a new one would take ages and the car would be unusable in the meantime. Jimmy Ronan started on Billy in his nasal whine: 'Is it ten or eleven children you have, Billy?'

'Ten.'

'Oh, God, how are they going to live? You won't survive that, you'll be sacked. You broke a Princess! That'll be lying around for months. We're talking about thousands and thousands of pounds ...'

This gnawed away in Wheatley's head until, in a rage, he ran down the factory to the foreman Billy Cunningham, caught him by the coat, pulled him up, pointed to the sump and said: 'You see that crack?'

'Yes?'

'Well, I put it there! It's all my responsibility. It's on my shoulders it rests.'

'Sure, we'll just order another one. What are you getting excited for?'

His relief was immense, but I always remember the straightforward way he took his responsibility and his refusal to accept fear. He'd be the type to take up his gun and go over the top of the trench.

That's what factory life was like. This idea that it was all bleak and awful, with no sense of fun, isn't true. I remember they used to play the *Music While You Work* programme, then decided to knock it off. We all started singing instead: people have to find a way to get through the day. A lot of that is lost in modern factories. When a shop steward called Paddy McGowan, who had a droll Dublin accent, came out from negotiations, crowds of people would slowly follow him to find out the outcome. He'd turn around, adjust his glasses, and say, 'My lips are sealed. Only nicotine can open them.' They'd all give him cigarettes, and he'd add, 'Nothing happened today.'

The United Irishman, the journal of the republican movement, circulated in the factory. It's also where I saw my first copy of *The Irish Socialist*, the only socialist newspaper being produced in Ireland at the time. In fact, it wasn't even produced in Ireland: it was printed in England because any printer who touched it here would have been picketed. I started reading the *Socialist* and found out about the Irish Workers' Party bookshop on Pearse Street. And then I decided that I'd better join the Communist Party.

I'd joined the library and was reading every anti-communist tract I could find: George Orwell, André Gide, Koestler's *The God That Failed*, the ex-communist Douglas Hyde, a book by a Jesuit called Ignace Lepp, *From Karl Marx to Jesus Christ*. I wasn't reading them because I wanted to be anti-communist but because, from their titles, they were books about communism. It's a comment on propaganda or ideas: if your disposition is such that socialism presents some set of answers to the difficulties you have in life, then no matter what the ideological superstructure tells you, you will find a way through it. Logically, I should have joined the anti-communist league, had there been such a thing, but I drew completely opposite conclusions.

I joined the party with a sceptical view of world communism. I knew it wasn't just an idealistic organization, but if you're going to organize to get rid of capitalism, you need armies, big forces, intellectuals, papers. And even though communism was quite small in Ireland, on a global scale they were the only show in town. I remember reading *36 Million Communists*

Say . . ., which came out in 1960 and claimed that, quite simply, if you could unite the people of the socialist world, the working class in the metropolitan countries and the national liberation movements, you could push back capitalism and open the door to socialism. Of course it didn't happen – the opposite did – but it wasn't an unreasonable proposition.

The gap between theory and reality is always strange. I asked Johnny Nolan behind the counter of the bookshop: 'This Irish Workers' Party – where do you join it?' Nolan, who was in his fifties at the time, was first involved in the socialist movement in 1923. I think he was born in a Comintern filing cabinet. He'd been through a long socialist life. He was an absolute ringer for Captain Mainwaring from *Dad's Army* and had the same mannerisms too. He was the most unrevolutionary revolutionary, a typical shopkeeper in a brown suit like you'd wear in a Catholic sodality, with a trilby hat and thick glasses. And he looks at me, while hardly looking at me at all, and says, 'I know nothing about them.' I didn't know what to say, so I bought a pamphlet by the British communist Harry Pollitt, *The Irish Socialist* and *Tribune*, the British left-wing paper.

But as I turn to leave, Johnny walks out to the door and says, looking up and down the road, 'We've been accused of a lot, but I wouldn't like to add kidnapping to it.' This might have been the beginning and end of my involvement with Irish communism. I wanted nothing to do with those cowards.

The Labour Party was never an option: it would be something to support and ginger up from the outside, but not to join. The only people in the party who impressed me were Owen Sheehy Skeffington and Justin Keating. Sheehy Skeffington was a Trot and didn't really belong in the party, and Keating was a communist – that was his real politics. It was their analytical tools, the way of thinking, that impressed me about the communists. You can always find a Labour TD who's very energetic, does this, that and the other, makes the right noises, but it's the wider perspective the communists bring, the measurement of history, seeing themselves along that trajectory, that impressed me. People in the Labour Party don't think like that. Some people from the Workers' Party moved to Labour, but by that time they had given up all belief in changing the world. It had been washed out of them; they had believed in the eastern European states rather than Marxism.

I began to read ferociously about communism and socialism, and to follow politics and debates. I had a peculiar attitude to the national question – I think I was a two-nations nationalist before there was such a theory. I saw it a bit like The Covey in O'Casey's *The Plough and the Stars*. 'What do you want to be raising that for? Let's have the origin, development and consolidation of the world proletariat,' that kind of thing, although reading Connolly would always pull you back a bit from that. But I was influenced as much by Seán O'Casey and George Bernard Shaw as ever I was by Connolly. When I was young everybody read Shaw: he understood Marx without being a Marxist, and was a great man for explaining him, without openly saying so.

I began attending the Catholic Workers' College, run by the Jesuits in Milltown, in 1962. There were classes on economics, social policy and so on. It was a big deal because it was plugged by the ITGWU as a counterweight to the People's College, which was backed by other unions. I didn't know about it at the time, or even about the People's College itself. The union paid you when you completed a course in the CWC. It was a time when many in the leadership of the trade union movement went over on scholarships to America, which were really CIA scholarships where anti-communism was the theme. The Catholic Workers' College fostered anti-communism. I attended a lecture on the Bolshevik revolution, which was the first time I came across names like Kerensky, but having read about the revolution independently I came to different conclusions to my lecturer's. All education has value, but there was a fair amount of propaganda in this particular one.

In 1964, before the passing of the Redundancy Payments Act, I worked in a job where a fella was laid off in the stores and I was asked to go down and cover for him. I refused because I wasn't getting the adult rate. Before this particular incident I would be sent down to do the work and I would go through the motions, but there were aspects I wouldn't do, like signing off. The foreman, O'Grady, would end up having to work alongside me and that would lead to hours' worth of effing and blinding. This Mexican stand-off went on for months. I wouldn't budge, and nor would the union. The shop steward, Noel Lambe, who lives around the corner from me and is still a friend, didn't have the same outlook as me or Billy Wheatley. He was more conservative and, while he never told me to do the work, he'd say, 'Could we not just get you a few more bob for doing it?' But I hung tough, O'Grady going mad at me every week.

I was young, fed up and sick of a country so backward in its outlook. Had the British stayed, I would have had access to an education. I've always resented not having an education, yet the movement educated me, and it was better in some ways because it was self-education. It was unstructured, though. I could have done with a bit more structure in the early days rather than just running into the library, taking everything with 'communism' or 'socialism' on the cover and reading in a haphazard way. But when I left Ireland in 1965, my feeling was one of bewilderment – a sullen, instinctual resentment that the state wasn't working. What I resented was the failure of the national revolution, not its success; what happened in Ireland in 1922 was a counter-revolution.

THREE

Every social group coming into existence on the original terrain of an essential function in the world of economic production, creates together with itself, organically, one or more strata of intellectuals …

Antonio Gramsci

In 1965 I went to England with Bernard Browne. We travelled on St Stephen's Day, when all the car factories were closed for the long holiday. I had very little money. We went to Luton first and then to Coventry, where a pal of Bernard's got us digs and showed us the lie of the land. When I first signed on the dole there, I said I wanted a job in a car factory. The man in the dole office said: 'I wouldn't take a job in a car factory. They have great money but they have so many strikes that they only end up with the average wage.' This did reflect a certain reality. There was full employment in England at the time and we soon got jobs in the General Electric Company.

There were 'Don't Run' signs all over the factory. 'The unions must be strong here,' I said to Bernard – Lincoln & Nolan were always trying to make you run! The biggest change was the money. I was getting the full rate of pay, £22 a week – a craftsman in Dublin would be getting about £9–10 at the time. I wasn't sending any money home because my father was dead, my mother died when I was sixteen and my sisters were working – it was quite a lot of money for drinking, gadding about the place and buying books.

The Cold War was ending and there was an expectation that the new Labour government in Britain would bring in some kind of socialism, or at least advance things. It's often forgotten that Harold Wilson won four elections, even if some of his periods in government were short. He certainly kept Britain out of the Vietnam War, despite considerable pressure. Later on, Tony Blair was scrambling to get into every war he could find alongside the Americans, but Wilson wouldn't do that because of the strength of the Left in the Labour Party and elsewhere.

I remember drinking in a pub in Coventry alongside a group of ten or twelve Labour councillors who were having a heated left-wing conversation. Infused with that was an intellectual tradition from Warwick University, people in both the Labour Party and the Communist Party: the only place with a similar, albeit stronger heritage of intellectual tradition in the UK at the time was Glasgow. Workers had great self-confidence. It was a very optimistic time in Britain.

The first thing Bernard and I did was join the Communist Party. They were delighted to have us: we were allocated a branch, accepted, and we went to a meeting where we met lots of Irish people including a man called Paddy Powell who was union convenor in Chrysler and later became an organizer for the ITGWU in Galway. The Irish Workers' Party produced a bulletin and he put me on the mailing list. I never came across the Connolly Association in Coventry.

Our Communist Party branch was great. Selling the *Daily Worker* was considered an honour for the members. There was a debate about changing the name of the paper to the *Morning Star*. I was in favour; it was about modernity, adjusting to things, reaching a wider audience. The party wanted to get the paper on as many shelves as possible and we were told to go to our local shop and ask for it, to insist they order two copies so that someone else might buy one.

But there were deeper issues going on during these debates. I had no position in the party other than that of a member, a spear-carrier looking up at the luminaries. We had theoreticians in the socialist movement then. I never hear anyone being called a theoretician these days, but these people were, not necessarily because they had been to university but because some of them worked in the car factory. They were organic intellectuals in Gramsci's sense. 'He's a theoretician of the party.' It was an honourable thing to say about someone.

Someone who made a deep impression on me was Harry Bourne – that's about one-third of his full name, because he was actually a Jew from Poland who had fought in the Spanish Civil War. There was a true internationalism in meeting people from diverse backgrounds with magnificent commitment to the Labour movement. I didn't always agree with Harry. He was a hard-line pea-green Stalinist. He was not in favour of changing the name of the paper: he wasn't in the camp that believed in adapting to the modern world. But it's completely wrong to see people like him as just apparatchiks doing the bidding of Moscow. The Stalinists' thought-out position was sectarian but it did carry the movement forward for a period. There were weaknesses in their analysis, but there was sacrifice and commitment too, and they weren't in people's pockets. People like Harry had gone through everything and put everything on the line.

A number of cultural events were going on at the time, including a film on the atom bomb called *The War Game*, banned by the BBC, which played in cinemas around the country. When I went to my local cinema the place was packed; everyone was handed a CND pamphlet on their way in. I also went to an anti-Vietnam war concert in the Belgrave Theatre where Ewan MacColl and Dominic Behan sang. There was a progressive atmosphere in Britain. The standard of living was higher than in Ireland and there was a greater sense of freedom. I embraced it all, choosing to interpret it as a result of the personal choices I made and the organization I joined.

20

There was a rich cultural and intellectual life in the Communist Party, particularly in its publications. I read the *Marxist Quarterly*, a fortnightly magazine called *Comment* and the *Daily Worker*. There were loads of pamphlets available on this, that and the other, with meetings about the various topics. This was not something I thought you'd get in the Labour Party.

The Communist Party launched a policy statement, 'The CP and Science'. One of the party's leading theoreticians, James Klugman, came to a meeting in Coventry and I'll always remember what he said: 'The Communist Party does not prescribe what scientists or artists should think or write. We tried that, and it was a disaster.' The party had given up the idea of directing art and science to suit a particular line and now believed in standing back. That didn't mean it had no critical interventions to make, but it wouldn't tell people what they must believe. The Lysenko affair was going on in the Soviet Union, interference of the crudest form in science and art, telling people how to think, what to research, what to write. As workers, we were encouraged to think about science as an alternative to all the religions around us.

Klugman once held up a copy of his 1951 book, *From Trotsky to Tito*, a compilation of every bit of mud the CP could throw at the Yugoslavs to prove they were betraying socialism. Klugman said that he put that book under his pillow every night to remind himself how wrong he could be. He knew he was writing rubbish, but he did it anyway. I was impressed by that willingness to admit his mistakes and learn from them.

We brought Klugman over to Ireland in 1968 and he went out to Maynooth to talk to novice nuns and clerical students. Paddy Carmody showed him all the papal encyclicals so he could address the progressive aspects of Catholicism. But Klugman said they were no use because the students didn't seem to be studying religion at all – they were all Maoists or Trotskyists!

The Communist Party had a Historians Group, which used to meet every week in London and discuss subjects such as the English revolution. Reports featured in the party paper. This went on for years, involving all the heavy hitters. They were completely free to argue any proposition they cared to put forward, precisely because nobody in the Soviet Union gave a tinker's curse what anybody thought about England in the 1640s. They could apply their minds creatively and the quality of the work that came out of the period at the time is impressive. You couldn't describe it as Stalinist dogma. It's genuine Marxist research of the highest quality, done collectively with continuous debate. The historian Eric Hobsbawm said he survived a lot of the problems in the party because of this; because he never dealt with the contemporary Soviet Union. I think he was very wise.

There was a good batch of Irish in the Communist Party, who certainly punched above their weight in the trade union movement. The TGWU convenor in the factory, Eddie Higgins from Cork, was in the party, and brought me along as a witness to his meetings with management. I'd sit there and absorb the atmosphere. These meetings had a proper purpose and an indirect purpose. The proper purpose might be the bonus scheme, or an individual grievance. The indirect purpose was what it said in that day's *Guardian* and *Daily Worker*. The debate would be like a ping-pong match between Eddie and the personnel officer. It was fascinating to listen to them discussing the questions of the day, particularly broad issues such as what the Labour government was going to do for industry.

I must have picked up a negotiating style from Eddie Higgins. He was conciliatory; rock solid but never stupidly aggressive. I'm not a believer in bull and bluster in negotiations. It's a technical skill; you have to come out with more than you go in with. The trick is subtraction from the sum total of the employer's wealth. Desmond Branigan, leader of the Marine Port and General Workers' Union, once told me that explaining to an employer why you should have a wage increase won't impress him at all. If he rationalizes why you shouldn't, you have to break that down, take his basis for rejection and destroy it. Industrial relations are an exercise in reason as well as power.

Harold Wilson was talking about incomes policy at the time and of course as soon as the guidelines came out the CP voted to try to break them.

A one-day strike was organized. In Ireland there would have been a discussion, but here in Britain Eddie just stood up and said, 'We're walking out. All in favour?' Hands went up and thousands of us walked out, just like that. There was no coercion, but no discussion or democratic participation either. In Ireland people would ask questions – perhaps the sheer size of the workforce precluded that.

A scandal had taken place a few years earlier over communists rigging elections in the Electrical Trades Union, but that had largely blown over and the party had expelled those involved. A Dublin man, Paddy O'Neill (who might have been on the London district committee of the ETU), told me that Harry Pollitt took them aside and warned them about ballot rigging: then, as they left the room, he shook each man by the hand and gave them a big wink. A lot of that sort of thing went on but it wasn't confined to the CP. There is a long tradition of forms of democracy being 'helped' by people on both Left and Right who were all convinced they had the right answer for the union.

The CP could have remained the major influence in the ETU but they didn't want 70 or 80 per cent of the power: they wanted it all. And to have it all, they took shortcuts, which came back and bit them in the arse, toppling the whole thing. The results were dreadful. Look at the role the ETU played in the 1984–5 miners' strike: had there been a progressive leadership in that union they would have won the strike. But all that was sacrificed. And the truth is that nothing would have stopped the talented communists with a record in that union from being elected: it was the untalented ones who did the damage.

The CP was faced with a choice of either keeping control of the ETU or democratizing it and being the main influence in it. They instinctively chose control over influence. While intellectually the party had abandoned Stalinism, pragmatically they still held on to parts of it. People with influence in a union don't want to let go. There's a narrow-minded attitude of just holding on and it didn't work for us. The Left really need to learn these lessons. It's not such a problem for Trotskyists because they don't have control or major influence in any unions, but if they ever do, they may well make the same mistakes. Shortcuts don't work.

I remember handing out communist leaflets outside mass in Coventry where Harry Bourne was standing in the 1966 general election. Irish lads didn't get a bad reception on the whole, mostly friendly indifference. I knocked on a door in Willenhall, and this huge fella – Desperate Dan multiplied by two – came out in his underwear, obviously worse for wear with drink, and said, 'What do you fucking want?' I told him who I was canvassing for and gave him the leaflet. He pulled it off me and said, 'Oh, great, I'll have a bit of that. There's no problem with nig-nogs in the Soviet Union.'

'I hope you went for him!' said Harry when I told him about the exchange. Maybe I have a sardonic way of looking at the world, but I thought it was both hilarious and awful. People in the party dressed me down for not responding to him gung-ho, but I had feared for my life. It shows the complexity of things.

Racism wasn't widespread, but it was certainly present. Enoch Powell legitimized prejudice but the CP and the unions did what they could to raise awareness of racism and combat it. Sometimes officials in the unions acquiesced and didn't confront it as they might have done. But you have to begin an educational process and judge where to make interventions and on balance the anti-racist cause in Britain was well served by the labour movement. I remember somebody in the party, maybe Harry, saying: 'There's only one race – the human race.' That's always stuck with me.

Harry Bourne didn't get many votes, but that was the electoral system and nothing to do with Harry. Conscious workers asked themselves, 'Do we want a Labour government or a Tory government? We're voting Labour. And the communists are there to keep Labour on the straight and narrow.' The CP tried to advance two things: one was the right to affiliate to the Labour Party and act collectively and democratically within that party. They lost that argument in the 1940s, but if it had happened it would have brought them right into the centre of things. If Labour can select candidates from the Fabian Society, why not from the Communist Party? After all, there was a Socialist League inside the Labour Party in the 1930s. The other was proportional representation: had there been PR in Britain, there would have been ten or twelve communist MPs in the House of Commons. The politics of the party was to use our influence inside the trade union movement to impact on the Labour government. That was where we put our weight and we didn't do too badly.

In 1966 Michael O'Riordan wrote an article on the Irish national question in *Comment* on the upcoming fiftieth anniversary of 1916. I was ambivalent about the national question in Ireland. This article made a big impact on me and I began reading more about imperialism and Ireland.

Being in England sharpened my sense of Irish identity in a way that would never have happened in Ireland. I became very conscious of people calling me Pat and developed a technique of always answering 'Yes, George?', which has stayed with me all my life. I wasn't being antagonistic and, in fact, without wanting to sound patronizing, some of my best friends are members of the English working class, people who would walk through walls for me, and that became very important later on.

I came home to Ireland during Easter 1966. The atmosphere was fantastic. The Irish Workers' Party released a very good publication on the fiftieth anniversary of the Easter Rising. Liam Mac Gabhann wrote a song about the Citizen Army to the tune of 'The Foggy Dew'. A television series called *Insurrection* on RTÉ portrayed news reporters going down to the GPO as if they were covering the events of Easter week. It was a terrific series and filled you with patriotic feelings.

And there was a working-class dimension to it all, with Connolly and the Citizen Army. It was the first time I read Lenin's estimation of the events. There was a revolutionary tradition in Ireland that probably wasn't new to people who had gone to secondary school and learned history, but they were new to me. A lot of people now say the anniversary celebrations were crude, but I reject that. There was a gap between 1916 and what people had done since, a gap that Fianna Fáil were trying to paper over.

I had two days off over Easter but ended up being away for the whole week. The three of us – myself, Bernard and Gerry Stafford – were all supposed to be suspended. I went into work completely dishevelled after the boat and a six-hour train journey. Needless to say, there was drink taken. The manager, a Galway man, grilled me and said: 'What were you doing?'

'I was celebrating the freedom of Ireland,' I replied.

'For seven days?'

'Yes.'

'Was it any good?'

'It was brilliant.' He gave me a big smile and told me to get to work. There was no question of being disciplined but had I been an Englishman I would have been sent up to be reprimanded at the very least.

The week back in Ireland shook me up. I went to a production in Birmingham of O'Casey's *The Plough and the Stars* with Peter O'Toole, Jack MacGowran and Siobhán McKenna and with the emotion of the whole thing I said to Bernard, 'I'm getting out of here. This isn't where I belong. If I'm going to make a contribution to this Marxist movement, I'd better do it in my own home place.'

I worked all the hours I could and saved about £300 because I knew I'd be facing unemployment in Ireland, and then I came home. Life wasn't terrible in England and I didn't experience anti-Irish feeling. It was more that Ireland was the place I would make my contribution. I had no plan for a job. I just came back. Had I stayed in England, instead of being sacked by Bill Morris, I might have become head of the TGWU.

FOUR

The only thing we ask of you is a commitment to support the trans-formation of property relations that took place in Russia in 1917, nothing else. The rest is doubtful ...

Paddy Carmody

I got off the boat from England one Saturday morning in 1966, took the train to Tara Street and went down to the party bookshop. Johnny wasn't there, but Mick O'Riordan was. I vaguely recognized him. 'I'm in the British party and I want to join the party here,' I said.

'Oh, that's great,' he said. 'When are you getting into harness? Are you looking for a job?'

My answer was fatally flawed. 'Am I fuck! I've got £300 and I'm going to piss it up against a wall first.'

I found out afterwards that he went to somebody else in the party and said, 'They'll let anybody into the British party. We'll have to keep an eye on him to see if he'll be any good or not.' But I was to develop a great friendship with Mick and a deep and abiding respect for him. We didn't always agree and fell out over loads of things – sometimes quite nastily – but he was the sort of man you meet once in a lifetime.

You'd think that going from the British party would be straightforward, but an interview was mandatory. There was never any doubt that I'd be admitted, it was more a case of 'If you have any questions, now's the time to ask them.' I don't believe that putting your name forward is all it takes to become a member of a party. You're making a commitment and there's no harm in ensuring that you know what you're doing.

It was a bright summer's day. Over in the party offices in Pembroke Lane three of us were being interviewed, myself, Bernard Browne and Billy Ebbs, a painter, who I didn't know. The panel consisted of Sam Nolan, Paddy Carmody and Michael O'Riordan. There was a general discussion covering the Soviet intervention in Hungary in 1956, ballot rigging in the ETU, the Berlin Wall and freedom inside the Warsaw Pact countries, the partition of Ireland and the national question, wages and unions.

Someone asked a question about partition: why were there two parties in Ireland, the Irish Workers' Party and the Communist Party of Northern Ireland? The answer was that this wasn't really the case – the division had developed during the Second World War. There might as well be one party and in the meantime a joint council did the job. The name Irish Workers' Party was coined because things were too difficult in the South to use 'communist'. It was a very practical explanation.

Another question related to the socialist countries. I didn't quite realize how integrated and international the Comintern had been. I was joining an Irish party, even though it was part of a world communist movement, and that was what attracted me. Paddy Carmody said something I've never forgotten:

> In this organization you will meet lots of people who will tell you lots of things about the Soviet Union. I liken it to Wolfe Tone and the French revolution. Wolfe Tone didn't write a letter every day approving of every person who had their head chopped off in the

French revolution. All that Wolfe Tone supported were the principles of the revolution: liberty, equality, fraternity. You are joining the communist movement and there are people who will tell you that you have to agree with some other party somewhere doing something. But the only thing we ask of you is a commitment to support the transformation of property relations that took place in Russia in 1917, nothing else. The rest is doubtful, contingent, changing, simply the to and fro of politics, and you don't have to go along with that. And don't mind people here who tell you that you have to, because you don't, and I don't.

Mick O'Riordan, sitting beside him like a man on a hive of bees, never said boo. I knew Paddy was making profound and thoughtful points. Had the world communist movement had that attitude it wouldn't have ended up in a heap. Paddy was a great thinker. I've met luminaries of the British CP including Palme Dutt and James Klugman and none of them would have the imagination and the integrity to come out with such a statement. I was impressed he wasn't trying to justify everything – quite the opposite, in fact. It was actually a stronger commitment than Mick's, who had a very different, more emotional relationship with the Soviet Union.

Paddy was challenging the idea of a centralized revolutionary movement, saying that change comes through the socialist movement grafting itself on to the revolutionary traditions in each land and then linking up with workers' struggles elsewhere. There's a difference between that and a world central committee telling everyone what to do. The Comintern became partly an appendage of the Soviet state.

James Connolly was trying to say that socialists should be the best patriots as well as internationalists; that these are not contradictory but complementary. People shouldn't be ashamed of being patriotic, particularly when they come from a small country. Some people might see Irish nationalism as something to be looked down on, but in truth it never had much aspiration beyond the Irish governing themselves. There was no imperialism, no wanting to dominate others. English or American nationalism is something else that creates national problems for others.

I knew these people's names from reading *The Irish Socialist* but Carmody confused me because he used to write under the name 'A. Raftery'. A health inspector with Dublin Corporation, he came back from holiday in Romania to find he'd been sacked. He took his case to the Amalgamated Transport Union – our union – and the official told him, 'Communists are banned in this union. We can't take up your case.'

Carmody went to the solicitor Con Lehane who wrote a letter for him that frightened the Corporation enough to take him back. He stayed in the union but wasn't impressed by the way they'd handled his case. And of course, if you ban communists in your union, what can you say when the Corporation starts to ban them too? We had a full-time official who was sacked from the TGWU, Andy Holmes, and we started a campaign to get him his job back in the shipyard. But the owner of Harland & Wolff said, 'Well, you sacked him. What do you expect me to employ him for? Good luck!' Where can you fault the logic of that?

Paddy Carmody's lectures were spellbinding, especially when he abandoned his notes. He always had copious notes but as soon as you saw them stuffed in the back pocket you knew you were in for a tour de force. Later, when I was deputy editor of *The Irish Socialist*, I used to go over to his house to help lay out the paper, but that was really an excuse. He would have it done already and we would have two bottles of stout, pig feet or some other meats, maybe a dram of whiskey, and we would just talk. He was a knockout character. I always felt that I was in the presence of someone quite special.

Mick O'Riordan and I spent a lot of time together. The party had a small printing press, which wasn't big enough for newspapers but we used to do pamphlets. Johnny Nolan was a printer, and I remember using the old metal type, working on election leaflets with Mick during the day, knocking on doors and distributing the leaflets at night. He had that street quality from having fought in Spain. I didn't know then the commendation he had won. He'd say he was always the first into battle and the last to leave and that his gun was equal to fourteen fascists. He was a great character, didn't take any prisoners and wasn't afraid of anything or anybody.

The Communist Party was the first place I ever met middle-class people. George Jeffares was middle class. His wife Marion Jeffares was a painter. After she died, I went up to see George and we had a few drinks. At one point he got up and looked around as if she were still alive and said that there few people knew the true rate of British casualties during the phoney war in 1939 because it was a protected secret. 'The prime minister knew, the cabinet secretary knew and Marion knew because she was secretary to the cabinet secretary. And do you know who else knew?'

'No, George,' I said. 'Who else knew?'

'Stalin knew, because she told him!'

I joined the Ireland-USSR Society for something to do. I thought it was a place where I could encourage people to sell *The Irish Socialist* but hadn't a clue what it really was.

'We should all sell *The Irish Socialist*! Tear down capitalism!' Frank's face was a picture.

Mick said, 'I want a word with you.' I was delighted – the General Secretary wanting to buy me a pint! – and met him at the bookshop in Pearse Street on a Friday afternoon. We went to a pub on the corner. After a couple of drinks he hesitated: I think what he wanted to say was something along the lines of, 'You have to leave the Ireland-USSR Society. You can't be going down there from Ballyfermot looking for people to sell *The Irish Socialist*.' But he couldn't do it, couldn't find the words, so he kept talking about everything and nothing until it was time for the last bus.

The next time I met Mick, he said, 'I'll have to have that conversation with you.' In the end, I think it was Paddy Carmody or Sam Nolan who just said, 'For Jesus' sake, will you get out of that Ireland-USSR Society, you're not welcome there!'

Running the bookshop for Johnny gave me unlimited access to books as well as a great variety of magazines such as the very profound *The New Hungarian Quarterly*. Johnny sourced Trotskyist theoretical magazines from America. He knew the battles going on in the youth movement and told me to have a look at them. 'But don't go showing them to everyone. It'll only confuse them.'

A good few people used to buy the *Daily Worker* there on a Saturday purely for the racing tips – it had a good sports page. There was a big row in the party about having a sports page but I always thought that if you wanted the paper to appeal to working-class people you had to have one. A paper has to have a commercial bent and although that sounds like terrible heresy, you have to be pragmatic. But some people in the party thought that encouraging people to gamble was terrible. They were like Methodists.

I was becoming aware of women's liberation. At that time there were no women in the car industry apart from the seamstresses who made the car seats. I once went for a drink in the Brian Boru after a republican parade with Madge Davison, a communist and a good friend. Women were not allowed in the bar. I said, 'It's all right, Madge. You go into the lounge and I'll bring you out a drink.' Her reply? 'If they did that to any other comrade, because he was black or a Protestant, you would have been outraged. You just said that so casually, Mick. You're a disgrace.'

We went somewhere else. Oscar Wilde said: 'The emotions of man are stirred more quickly than man's intelligence.' I thought I understood women's liberation but got the dig in the mouth I deserved and it knocked me down. I developed a more empathetic view after that, which was to help me later on because I represented thousands of women in equal pay cases. Madge worked at Gallaher's cigarette factory, qualified as a lawyer later and was involved in the civil rights movement but died young from cancer. She was from the Protestant community and a great Irish republican.

Years later we did a retrospective at the Desmond Greaves School on 1969 and the civil rights movement. Michael Farrell spoke. One woman recalled that she asked him about women's liberation and he had replied: 'No, no, no, we've got to sort out a united Ireland and socialism first.' He was very apologetic when, decades later, she reminded him about what he'd said.

I was on the executive of the Irish Workers' Party from 1967 and then went on to the political committee, which was extraordinary because I was probably the first new person for twenty or thirty years. Everybody else was ancient. Ireland had been a difficult place for communism in the 1950s. I was only elected because Joe Deasy's wife, Patricia Hayden, was dying of cancer and had to leave the committee. Mick put his hand on my shoulder and said, 'You're being elevated to the political committee.' I felt fantastic.

There was a second tier of leadership, people like Johnny Mooney, Johnny Montgomery, Packie Early and Sam Nolan, who'd been around the block a few times. There were also crackpots in the party, people who'd give you a pain in the ear. Some would repeatedly tell you not to watch UTV because it had adverts and would then report you to the central committee if they thought you did. They were generally laughed at, though.

I vaguely remember the 1954 election campaign, and my mother arguing with my uncles over Mick O'Riordan, who was better known than any other candidate. All over the country, bishops and other candidates were talking about him. He used to tell a story about his nomination. Brendan Behan and Johnny Mooney signed his papers, which had to be in by noon. He went over to City Hall and handed them in, but the Corporation official said, 'No, I'm rejecting that. There's no Brendan Behan in this constituency. There's a Brendan Francis Behan.' Mick went back round to the pub with a fresh form, but Behan was gone. Johnny signed, and Mick himself signed 'Brendan Francis Behan'. Then he got a drop out of a pint and smudged the signature a bit. When the man from the Corporation saw that, he said: 'Typical Behan!' and accepted the papers.

In a way, what we brought to the party was a challenge to all that. Survival mode was the main thing I encountered and the habits of ten or fifteen years, when sheer survival was a victory, had to be broken. When the Connolly Youth Movement (CYM) was founded in 1967, we changed those habits, getting the party involved in agitation. While I wasn't actually a founding member of the CYM, in practice I was because they'd just had one meeting before I joined. I was the chairman later. In fact, I didn't want to get involved in youth politics, I wanted to stay in the party and be involved in the trade union movement. But Mick O'Riordan prevailed upon me to become involved in the CYM. By that time he must have changed his attitude towards me and seen me as trustworthy!

The CYM wasn't a communist organization but a communist-influenced organization full of Trotskyists, Maoists, independents, all kinds of people. It was fairly large – a few hundred young people – and we took up lots of issues: picketing the Department of Education over the price of schoolbooks, picketing building sites over safety for apprentices. The CYM wasn't affiliated to the Communist Party and its constitution was deliberately pluralistic, stating that the Irish revolution and Irish socialism would be built by a multiplicity of forces and traditions including republicanism, the Far Left and others. I wrote the constitution, lifting it to some degree from a document by the Australian youth league, and also recognizing the special position of individuals as well as parties, people like Peadar O'Donnell and Wolfe Tone. That was obviously Paddy Carmody's influence, as I realized later.

The CYM held a debate between myself and Manus O'Riordan over the events in France in 1968. In a packed-out room, I chinned Manus by two or three votes: he made a very rational case for a revolution in France but I was supporting the CP line, which wasn't as revolutionary as that. I remember saying that the French Communist Party was known as 'the party of the dead' because of what the Gestapo did to them in the Second World War. I had read about that and it struck me deeply. They started the resistance movement and were murdered in their thousands, and I was asking people to give the party of the dead the benefit of the doubt.

The Maoists gave us the most problems. I had a row with a Maoist who absolutely upheld Stalin, denied the twentieth congress of the Soviet Communist Party where Stalin had been denounced and called Khrushchev a revisionist and destroyer of communism. That was the tenor of the debate. The Chinese communists were critical of the French, Italian and Yugoslav parties, but they were really surrogates to criticize the Soviet Union. The Socialist Party today represents exactly the kind of tradition upheld by the Maoists in those days. They were absolute Stalinists of the 'class against class' period, putting their ideas forward with utter simplicity: socialism versus capitalism, all the good guys on one side and the bad guys on the other. They were real hardliners.

Six of that crowd were brought before an open meeting. They made an argument that Bernard Browne shouldn't be in the chair because he was biased. 'But I'm not going to vote,' said Bernard.

'Doesn't matter! We want the chair.'

'OK, but the chair isn't voting.'

'We don't care, we want the chair.'

'OK.'

They got the chair and we won by one vote. Afterwards I said to one of them: 'You may think you're a Stalinist, comrade, but Stalin would never have done that!'

Six Maoists were thrown out of the movement. Splits are often inevitable, but they're not a good idea. It's always worth looking for other ways of doing things.

Ken Coates, who was involved with the Institute for Workers' Control in Britain, said that every split in the movement represents a partial truth; and if you could fuse them all together you would get a whole truth. There is a religious connotation to Marxism, the idea that, if only those of us who are reading this book correctly get together against those who are reading it upside down, then we'll get there quicker. Thinking like that takes up a ferocious amount of people's time and energy. There has to be a better way to keep these movements together, but without an answer we won't be able to change the world. It seems like an abstraction, but it's actually quite urgent, particularly in Ireland. Capitalism is in deep trouble, and the socialist movement is so sectarian that it's eliminating itself. There doesn't appear to be any capacity to forgive and forget now that the Soviet Union is over. Would people fall out over different interpretations of the French Revolution? So why fall out over the Soviet Union? And yet that's still mulling around the movement.

The CYM later became a Young Communist League. We had to discuss a merger with the YCL in the North and ran into trouble about what to call it. While the name Connolly Youth had a certain appeal in the Republic, there were difficulties with it up there where it might cut you off from the culture of Protestant youth. We won that debate, but I'm not sure it was a tactical victory.

About fifteen CYM people went on to become senior union officials. It's interesting that none of us were successful in electoral politics, but at that time the industrial working class was more important than now. The weakening of industry has also weakened a certain type of working-class organization, so trade unionists have to be more political to be effective. We were political, but it was struggle at the point of production, as we used to call it.

I went to a YCL school in Hastings with young communists from all over the world. At that time the British party used to take quite an interest in the colonial world. My fare over was paid and Mick gave me an extra £20, saying, 'That's to look after yourself while you're over there and to buy a drink at the bar.' I was in the UK for about a week. Johnny Campbell, one of the Red Clydeside shop stewards during the First World War, gave a lecture. Palme Dutt spoke – he was a brilliant man and a very competent speaker. James Klugman was there, as well as young communists from Kenya, the Sudan and Indonesia, which had a huge Communist Party until they were wiped out by Suharto. The word 'eye-opener' doesn't do justice to how I felt to be among these people. They wanted to change the world. I was fascinated by what they were trying to do but I was worried about fitting in.

FIVE

In 1963 a house collapsed in Fenian Street, killing a number of children, and the demolition of other tenements put tremendous pressure on housing. Dr John O'Connell ran a campaign around Marshalsea House in Bridgefoot Street. Sinn Féin were involved in a campaign against attempted evictions in Sarah Place in Islandbridge. The housing situation in Dublin during the sixties and seventies was chronic.

The British Labour government bringing in extra taxation on profits made as a result of rezoning – taxation which should have been brought in here, as the Kenny report later said – brought it all to a head. A lot of hot money came in from Britain, money for building offices rather than housing. This pushed a lot of houses out of the private sector and exacerbated the crisis. There were a certain number of empty houses too, because owners were getting rid of tenants so they could sell to developers.

We started the Dublin Housing Action Committee in 1967. Sinn Féin, the Irish Workers' Party, branches of the Labour Party, the British and Irish Communist Organization were affiliated, as were individuals like Hilary Boyle and Fr Michael Sweetman. We demanded the declaration of a housing emergency and a report on housing in the long term. We started to attract homeless people, the only people with a vote in the campaign. The rest of us had no vote, so there would be a contestation trying to influence the homeless. We had an invaluable asset in Bernard Browne, who was both a communist and homeless, which gave him a lot of street cred. This pivotal figure, chairman of the campaign, squatted in a place in Mountjoy Square.

On a day he was supposed to be evicted we got the place ready to face the sheriff. A carpenter, Liam Mulready, fixed a brace to the door, which meant that to break down the door you would have to break down the wall. We scattered marbles on the stairs. We intended to torch the place and had rope ladders to escape. There were hundreds of people outside. The sheriff came along, took one look at it and just fucked off. It shows how proper planning has its place in the world of agitation.

There were loads of sit-ins. I remember a big one in the Custom House, and Mick O'Riordan being pulled down the steps by two young gardaí with a hold on his legs. Seán Dunne successfully hid in a cupboard. There were huge amounts of activity. We once protested at de Valera as he went to mass in the Pro-Cathedral, with placards saying: 'House the homeless'. There were months and months of frenetic activity.

When a couple of hundred of us occupied College Green a garda caught me by the sleeve, which came right off in his hands, and he fell arse over tit. I took to my heels but wasn't very fit and didn't get too far. I ran into Mulligan's pub, hung up my coat and went into the toilet. I waited for a while, then came out and bought myself a pint. Some of the other demonstrators came in and told me some people had been arrested. They said we should go to the station and protest about that, but I was just happy to have got away with it and didn't want to get recognized. I got slagged as a coward, which was fair enough. I had a few more pints, and then I had to work out how to go home without my one-armed coat being noticed. So I just took someone else's coat off the rack, put it on, and walked home. On another occasion there was a confrontation on O'Connell Bridge during a big protest, and the riot squad left a lot of people worse for wear. They batoned us, although I made sure to stay out of their range

I once met the Fine Gael front bench when they were in opposition and Liam Cosgrave was speaking about a housing emergency. Some people thought we shouldn't talk to people like that on principle, but I never took that view. He was a public representative. You have to campaign for everybody's support whether you believe in them or not, and I was glad that the Fine Gael front bench were supporting us.

The demonstrations were huge, but we were running the campaign on a wing and a prayer. The IWP would do leaflets for us on a Gestetner duplicating machine, or Sinn Féin would do bits and pieces for us, but it was a ramshackle organization. Homeless people began to get involved. We took over a hotel with three or four families around the Baggot Street area, a small, upmarket place: nothing is too good for the workers! We had to break down the door. There's always a reluctance to do something like that but we were getting it through to people that these were necessary measures.

Once the campaign gained traction we came across all kinds of problems, most of which we were ill-equipped to deal with. I remember being told about incest in a family and spoke to people who said we should alert social services – but the family wanted the DHAC to deal with it. We were mining into a seam of issues just below the housing crisis that fed directly into it.

Dennis Dennehy, secretary of the DHAC, went to jail. Dennis could be quite sectarian in his politics, and some of the things he wanted us to do were a bit wild. I liked him as an individual but he wasn't the greatest tactician in the world. I said to Bernard, 'This is great now. With Dennis in jail, he won't be able to suggest anything. The problem is that if we get him out, he'll be back in the campaign again.' Dennis used to say he was a Maoist and a Stalinist, but in his heart he was an anarchist. In jail for squatting, he started a hunger strike, then a hunger and water strike, and collapsed. He was given a mobile home just off Queen Street with water and electricity, having been living in a caravan at the bottom of Sarsfield Road: one whole side of the caravan was taken up with a photograph of Mao.

His was a personal victory. Labour TD Michael O'Leary was involved in raising the money, as was Victor Bewley of the café family. Bewley was ethically supportive of the Housing Action, but people like O'Leary were afraid of it. A person who impressed me no end, because he never missed a meeting of the campaign, was Fr Michael Sweetman. He never resorted to violence – although he would sit in occasionally – and always stood up for us when we were in trouble. We were occupying Bernard's place overnight when he told us all about yoga: I learned yoga from the Jesuits – about the only thing I did learn from them!

There was a split on the committee in 1970 over how to manage the eviction of squatters. Many of the republicans were keen on confrontation, but not in the way that was suggested. Séamus Costello wanted to confront it almost in military fashion. My attitude was that if you were forced to vacate a house, the important thing was that the television cameras see the family being taken out. If they just found a lot of politically dedicated people defending the house, that would justify the propaganda being made against us. It should be the families there, with the rest of us only blocking outside. They occupied a house in Pembroke Road and they were intent on defending it. Mick O'Riordan, Bernard and I had a row with them over that, and we left the house. The police moved in and the television cameras arrived, but there weren't any homeless people, which was disastrous. I'm not against using physical force in the cut and thrust of confrontation, but I didn't think it was wise for us to be in the house that way.

I was asked if I was prepared to hand up the house, and my answer was yes. It was better to fail if we couldn't get a family to occupy it. We, the movement, had no houses. The DHAC was a movement supporting home-less families who needed houses and occupied them. That's a militaristic concept, as if ceding the house were ceding territory to the enemy. The idea that us revolutionaries would take the house was barren.

Republicans were very active in the campaign, particularly in social agitation after the failure of the IRA campaign in the 1950s: Seán Ó Cionnaith, Máirín de Búrca, Seán Dunne, Cathal Goulding in the background, Éamonn Walsh, who later became a Labour TD in Tallaght. Individual Labour TDs supported us: O'Leary, for example, because a lot of the occupations took place in his constituency. But he was semi-detached, in and out: if there was a photograph to be taken or a baby to be kissed, he'd always be there. The person who really attacked us, and introduced the Forcible Entry Act to repress us, was Kevin Boland, who later became a rip-roaring republican but was then going through a very authoritarian phase. I later spoke on platforms with him on other issues, but that's the way he was then.

There was support from the Dublin Council of Trade Unions and from individual trade unionists. The Trades Council was represented by Séamus Geraghty, who allegedly brandished a small silver gun at a meeting outside the GPO and said, to great cheers, that he was representing the Dublin working class. Mattie Merrigan spoke for us, as did Mickey Mullen of the ITGWU, but we never got into the sinews of the trade union movement.

I first met Mattie for the DHAC, before I was in the union. I just walked into the ATGWU office saying I wanted to meet the General Secretary and was taken in to meet him. Mattie gave me a brusque, 'What do you want?'

'I want a resolution at Dublin Trades Council,' I said.

'Done.'

'I want you to talk to the Labour Party.'

'Done. Do you want anything else?'

'I want you to speak.'

'Done.'

And it was all done. He scribbled a few notes and I was out of the office in ten minutes, but everything he said happened and he even sent me a letter outlining what we agreed. Not a lot of officials are like that.

The DHAC created a huge level of mood music in the background, and two things came out of it: the declaration of a housing emergency and the Kenny report of 1974. The Kenny report is still an important document. I remember raising it years later in the partnership talks, and people yawning whenever I mentioned it, but it addressed much of the housing crisis, making sure that people don't make money out of planning decisions. It recommended that the state could buy land at its use value plus 25 per cent, which was eminently doable. It has never been implemented because every government since has claimed it would be unconstitutional. I don't believe it would be. Kenny was a High Court judge, and High Court judges don't usually recommend things that are unconstitutional. There is a clause in the Irish constitution, put there by Comrade de Valera, and it talks about private property not being used to damage 'the common good'. That's quite a socialistic clause if it is interpreted properly by a leftist government. It may violate a whole load of EU treaties, but it's good to have it in the constitution, though you never hear anyone talk about it. It shows how left wing Fianna Fáil was in the 1930s.

Governments could have tested that proposal in the Kenny report, but it suited them not to. That would have dealt with land banks and the housing crisis we have today. In the long term nothing was done, but this was down to the failure of the Labour Party and the Left to fight for a solution. In the short term a lot of houses were built, so it was a successful agitation.

I first met Mary early in January 1968 in a dance hall where the garda station now stands on Harcourt Street. It was originally called the Four Provinces and belonged to the Bakers' Union, but after its sale it became the Television Club. It had murals of Mexican peasants by Diego Rivera up and down the hall. Mary had a lovely face, and I asked her to dance. I walked her home to Inchicore. We came from very similar working-class backgrounds. She seemed to think I was funny, which was a help. On the Monday night we went to see *The Family Way* with Hayley Mills in the Inchicore cinema. The Soviet Union is gone, Fianna Fáil has collapsed, the Labour Party is facing oblivion and the Communist Party is not the force it once was, but our relationship has survived and flourished over all those years.

I wasn't a very promising prospect. Once the rent was paid out of my thirty-eight shillings dole, it didn't leave a lot for going out dancing. I only had temporary work since returning from England, and it looked like that was all I would ever have: live horse and you'll get grass, as the saying goes.

Those years were quite precarious. I went through periods of despair when I thought I'd never get a job. For her to take me on she had to be committed to me in a completely unselfish way, because I must have been the most unappealing prospect from a financial point of view. She certainly wasn't taking on an asset, but someone with strong liabilities.

Mary had a knowledge of and interest in politics. She had scant time for the Communist Party. She liked the people in it and got on with them but she considered it a kind of sect. It never divided us and she never told me to leave the party, but she certainly regarded it as a bit off the wall. I always thought it was very important to have a life outside the party – that way you can keep your critical faculties and you wouldn't be doing something because there was no other avenue available to you.

Mary introduced me to music and artists like Janis Ian, all of whose records she had, and The Beatles, with whose music she was very familiar. We shared a love of cinema, and went to Belfast to see *MASH* two weeks before it came out in Dublin.

We were married in August 1972 in St Michael's Church on Emmet Road. I had to be interviewed by the parish priest because I had been quite open about my beliefs. I got on with him: he had a fondness for the drink, and he didn't seem to take the pomp and circumstance of the Church too seriously. He had a complete understanding of my situation, and said there'd be no problem, that he'd sort things out with the archbishop. I had heard of communists having problems getting married in church, but it never occurred to me not to do so. I didn't see myself as a crusader imposing my beliefs on others, and I just conformed to the norm as it was then. I didn't give it much thought, and assumed it was something Mary would have wanted for the sake of her family. Years later she told me she wasn't hung up about it at all.

The reception was in the Finglas Inn and we went to Whyte's Hotel in Wexford for a few days for our honeymoon. By the end of the week I had no money at all, and when we got back to Dublin on the Friday Mary's father gave me a very welcome fiver. So we went to see *The Godfather*, which I had read on honeymoon. Mary had a job in the civil service, and, of course, when a woman in the civil service got married in those days she had to give it up. We set up home together in Ballyfermot. Having the house on a flat rent was a great advantage for us and we eventually bought it.

Louise was born in September 1973. She was ill for a while and spent time in St Ultan's Hospital. She was in there at the time of the big Loyalist bombings of Dublin in 1974 and we had to walk over to see her because the buses weren't running. Dublin was like a morgue. I was in the union office on Marlborough Street when the first bomb went off the day before, and I remember the boom of it. Suzanne was born in February 1979.

I never 'fell' in love with Mary: it was more of a slow-burning, lasting love. Her commitment to me and the family has been extraordinary. I said at Suzanne's wedding that I had spent my life trying to change the world and been spectacularly unsuccessful, but that Mary had been spectacularly successful at rearing our children. Louise became a very competent union official and is now a Sinn Féin TD and Suzanne is a deputy principal in a school in Neilstown. I have four grandchildren now, and a great-grandchild.

SIX

The spontaneity I exercised the day I threw away my Communion coat was, to some degree, knocked out of me in the Communist Party, and I learned to substitute discipline in its place. There's nothing wrong with that; there's not much you can do without discipline. Discipline replaces some of that spontaneous rebelliousness, and that's inevitable if you're going to change the world and manoeuvre against people with power who can destroy you if you make mistakes, but there was also a loss involved. I have often asked what happened to the young fella with a pure sense of justice.

There's always a tension between spontaneity and discipline but I was lucky because I joined the Communist Party at a time when there was huge questioning over that very thing. To be a Stalinist then was to be isolated, laughed at and marginalized, but I didn't realize how deep the roots of authoritarianism still were. My earliest battles in Ireland were with the Maoists, refuting the Stalinist arguments line by line and expressing the orthodox communist view against them. There was a great strength in the communist movement honestly admitting its mistakes, something the great religions of the world have never done. But I overestimated the changes taking place.

In the lead-up to the Czech events in 1968 there was an argument about whether we would publish the reform programme of the Communist Party of Czechoslovakia in *The Irish Socialist*. Paddy Carmody and I wanted to publish it, as did Sam Nolan and George Jeffares. A few people were against it. Seán and Lillie O'Rourke were totally against it, some were equivocal and others just thought it was too much space in the paper to give to a foreign issue. But Mick O'Riordan was strongly in favour. The party used to produce a weekly bulletin. There were bylines, but members of the executive wrote it in rotation and I used to follow Mick. The Soviet and the Czech communist parties had a meeting in 1968, and the Soviets were doing tank manoeuvres nearby at the same time, showing them their weapons. Mick O'Riordan condemned this in the bulletin.

But when the shit hit the fan and the tanks went in to Prague, he had just been away on holiday in either the Soviet Union or Poland and came back with a different line, supportive of the Soviets. The same thing happened with Betty Sinclair, a leading member of the CPNI. But the communist parties North and South condemned the Soviet intervention. In the CYM I had to use my casting vote on the executive to condemn it. The membership was more clearly against it, by about 60–40. It was narrow, and there were strong feelings. There was an attempt to get party members who were asleep back on their feet and vote against us, and people we hadn't seen for a while turned up. It created a terrible division. Trust was broken down. It had a huge, negative impact in the party.

I never thought the vote would go the other way. The only place in which the party had serious influence was in the unions. We were not an electoral force at all. And, unlike Britain where the industrial people were all 'tankies', in Ireland all the 'revisionists', so to speak, were industrial people: me, Carmody, Sam Nolan who was secretary of Dublin Trades Council, were all totally opposed to the Soviet leadership. There wasn't a big intellectual section in the party, but the people who were effectively working in the trade union movement were mostly opposed. There were some exceptions: Noel Harris, who was an official in the Association of

Scientific, Technical and Managerial Staffs, was very pro-intervention, and I remember having a row with him over it. In the North the only significant communist opposed to us was Betty Sinclair. Everybody on the political committee bar Mick was against what was done, although the executive was a bit different. It never crossed my mind that we would lose the debate.

But after that, what do you do? Do you call for the overthrow of the state? There was really no point in getting into that because it wasn't going to happen. We had to hold the party together for things where we could make a contribution and stay away from other discussions – a kind of escape into pragmatism, really.

Johnny Nolan was on holidays when the intervention in Czechoslovakia took place. We had a meeting and every vote counted, so somebody was deputized – Sam Nolan, I think – to ring him and find out what his stance was. 'I haven't got one. I'm not required to have one. I'm on holidays.' I now wonder what he was at. If there are two factions and you don't join either, both of them are going to be after you wanting to get you on side and keep you sweet. I also think he believed the intervention was a disaster, but that condemning it wasn't such a bright idea either. I never found out Johnny's position.

He had seen so much. He came into the bookshop once during a military dispute between China and Vietnam and said, 'Remember that book I gave you on internationalism? Well, you can tear it up because there's nobody else reading it!' This is a guy who had been in the movement for years and seen everything. I asked him once what Larkin was like, and he told me: 'He was an impossibilist. It was impossible to work with him, and impossible to work without him.'

He told me he once stopped off in London on his way to a Comintern meeting and was asked how many Trotskyites the Irish party had expelled. 'None,' he replied, 'we haven't got any.'

'Oh, they'll never believe that,' the CP man said to him. 'Tell them you've got rid of half a dozen.' And he did.

Johnny never gave up on his revolutionary beliefs, but what he said in 1968 made sense. Of course, he didn't want to fall out with people, but he was also not in a hurry to put himself into a position. I wrote an article in the paper about Gerry Fleming, who was in the painters' union and later became a rights commissioner. Johnny called me in to the back of the shop and said, 'Would you stop writing that bloody nonsense! Get away from all that and stick to what you know, the trade union movement. That's what will change things here.' And he was totally right.

There was a big debate in the European Marxist and communist movement about problems that people as far back as Karl Kautsky and Eduard Bernstein had tried to resolve. How do you advance to Marxist socialism through democratic means under capitalism in an advanced democracy? There's not going to be a revolutionary road like there was in Russia. And you have to give the working class a principled perspective so they can trust you if you come to power. You have to explain what democratic means of struggle you'll apply when you have state power. The idea of pluralism – and elections you can lose as well as win – has to be taken into account. A big part of dealing with that is what you might call communist jurisprudence; how you administer justice in a diverse socialist country. How do you guarantee a diverse media and publications? We were interested in all these questions.

Other than the argument about moving to a more democratic form of socialism, there was, for me, the fundamental question about the right of nations to self-determination, which was the absolute and utter clincher. Self-determination couldn't be qualified, but that's what the Brezhnev doctrine did. There's nothing going for Brezhnev's argument at all. It comes down to the idea that the Soviet Union, as the first socialist power, had the right to intervene wherever it wanted.

I thought that if we had an ambiguous, mixed attitude to that on this island, we would be finished, with no credibility whatsoever. We were one of the few European nations to have been colonialized systematically over hundreds of years and have fought in every way for independence. Most other European countries were imperialist themselves. If you take the case of the Scottish and the Welsh, to some degree their ruling classes got into bed with the English, whereas ours was half in and half out. That made colonialism worse for us.

And then you had Czechoslovakia, that little country beside a big country. In all the arguments I had with Mick O'Riordan he would point out things that I might not like about Czechoslovakia, for example, that they were prepared to accept some unemployment. But the question is, can you deal with problems by suppressing them, by pretending that there are no problems, just the forward march of socialism? If I wanted to make him uncomfortable – as I often did – I just had to bring the topic round to little countries and big countries. Did the Soviet intervention mean we had to let the Brits tell us what kind of socialism we could have? Well, then Mick was in deep trouble.

He would get away with it by saying, 'The Soviet Union is different.' How can you get into the head of somebody like that? When he was fighting in Spain, equipment, food, guns, everything he had that worked came from the Soviet Union. While everybody else just talked, they did something.

For me there was no debate. The British, Italian, Dutch, Swedish, French, Spanish and Chinese parties were all against the Soviet intervention – even La Pasionaria, the famous Spanish communist actually living in the Soviet Union. Maybe the international communist movement never got over the split.

I went in to Tim Young's pub in Ballyfermot to sell *The Irish Socialist* one night just after the Soviet intervention. A fella said, 'I'll have that.' I gave him a paper and told him it was fourpence. He dropped four pennies on the floor one by one in front of everyone. I picked up the money, and as I was going he said, 'Wait, I want to show you something.' He tore the paper up, threw it on the ground and said, 'Get out, you commie bollocks.' Then the manager came out and told me, 'You're a fucking troublemaker. Don't sell that paper in here anymore!'

What happened in 1968 was shocking, especially since I had been arguing that the Soviet Union would never do anything like this. Statements and books were put out claiming that Czechoslovakia was abandoning the fundamental tenets of socialism. And of course, if you take the lid off something, people will say all sorts of things, but that was no justification for the Soviets doing what they did. If you could pick your battles you'd always win them, but they come out of nowhere and you are made by your response to them. It's partly what makes us human: we have to grapple with things and find an honest way through.

I've never wavered in my view about the invasion of Czechoslovakia. It was even worse than Hungary in 1956. Hungary had been a fascist state and there were reactionary forces around, but that wasn't true of Czechoslovakia, which had a modern, advanced working class and where the Communist Party was in control. Would it have ended up in some kind of mish-mash between communism and social democracy? Probably, and that would have been better. Ultimately, if you wanted – as I did – the conditions where we could advance the cause of socialism in western Europe, you had to look at that as opening the door to a transformative process in the Soviet Union itself. If there was less danger of war or invasion, then all the apparatus of repression that existed in the Soviet Union had less justification, and resources could have been shifted into making communism a more human experience for the people, spending as much on cars and washing machines as they did on tanks and AK47s.

Mick O'Riordan would have agreed that, ultimately, somebody needed to go in and dismantle the Soviet Union. And I was naive in not being prepared to defend socialism. Towards the end of 1968 people looked at the idea of getting rid of Mick but we didn't seriously consider getting another general secretary and it looked like he would reluctantly go along with the decision. It's only now I realize that he never did – that he was working against it from the early days.

He broke every meaningful tenet of democratic centralism in his quest to reverse what he considered an unprincipled decision. How could he have stood everything he believed in on its head and worked against the Soviet Union? But that's what would have been expected of him. The fact that he, who believed in democratic centralism, didn't practise it shows that there's something wrong with the doctrine itself.

Democratic centralism does not stand up. I've read the recollections of people who were far more influential than me in the communist movement who have come to the same conclusion. Imagine if you take a certain view of something but the organization votes for another – then you would have to disbelieve what they believe. You can't ask someone to believe what they don't because of a vote. There's room for looseness, which doesn't mean weakness.

It's one thing to join the communist movement and sign up to democratic centralism as a method, but it's quite another thing to apply it to jurisprudence and running nations. It has been disastrous. In a place the size of the USSR, how could everyone change step at the same time? I'm not saying leadership doesn't matter or that Lenin didn't have a point, but the application of his principles has to be fundamentally reviewed. We have to be honest about structures that ask people to do things that are impossible for them. Something that's so easily and regularly abused has to have something fundamentally wrong with it. Whether in government in eastern Europe, in big communist parties or in small left-wing sects, once democratic centralism is used against you there's no way back.

Unions don't have democratic centralism, but they get things done. When someone passes a picket, the union tries to crush them: you don't allow freedom of conscience when there's a strike on. To save our individuality we have to use our collective strength. We have a discussion, come to a decision and everyone respects that. But I've never heard anyone in a union talk about democratic centralism. Before Lenin existed, things got done and Marx didn't have a doctrine of democratic centralism.

There's no doubt that Mick worked against the party's decision. We weren't up to taking the job off him but in retrospect it's what we should have done to keep the party in line. No one else wanted the job – the pay wasn't very good, for a start – but someone else might have been able to do it, Sam Nolan or Paddy Carmody, say. The North was blowing up and our preoccupation was with that situation, where we were a major player in the civil rights movement. Mick had a very good, principled position on the North. He was a great Irish republican.

But there were always internal divisions. People judged you, not on the practicality or quality of the idea you were putting forward, but on whether you were soft or hard on the Soviet Union. It became endemic, determining whether you were a 'real' communist or not. If you demanded a pay increase in work, you were only saying it because you were anti-Soviet or pro-Soviet. This kind of idiocy ultimately destroyed the Communist Party.

SEVEN

... to transform the dry detail work of trade union organization into the constructive work of revolutionary Socialism, and thus make of the unimaginative trade unionist a potent factor in the launching of a new system of society ...

James Connolly

I applied for a job through a box number in *The Sunday Press*, which turned out to be in the Semperit tyre factory on Killeen Road. A few days later I got a letter from the recruitment company vetting the applications. I wish I'd kept it. It said: 'Thank you for your application. We will not require your services now or ever.' That was fairly straightforward, anyway. And why wouldn't they say that? Chairman of the CYM, on the executive of the Irish Workers' Party, writing in *The Irish Socialist*, appearing on all kinds of demonstrations, occasionally quoted in the press – what chance had I of a job?

I had been unemployed since coming back from England, apart from odds and sods including making blocks out in Feltrim – very hard work for two or three months in the summer, getting the bus at 6.30 am – and then summer work in Baxendale's builders' providers on Capel Street. I got a temporary job for the ESB, digging a hole in Baggot Street for a cable, where everyone was from Kilkenny except for me. I was wearing the only suit I possessed and they wanted me to start straight away, even though I didn't have working clothes on. I jumped into the hole to get the shovel, but when I hit the ground I became dizzy and collapsed for lack of food.

This took place near the party office and every morning Mick O'Riordan would get off the bus to talk to me while I was working. All the Kilkenny fellas were wondering about this friendly man in a suit. On the last day of work, about six weeks later, I went for a drink with them. 'Are you a company spy?' one of them finally asked.

'No! Why?' I replied.

'That fella from the ESB you were talking to every day!'

I went to join the ATGWU but they wouldn't let me in. 'Ah, it's no use, you'll only be there for six or eight weeks.' Back then it was common. There was a story about a caretaker in the Workers' Union of Ireland, and when people came to join he'd say, 'No, you can't join the union. It's full.' He just didn't want the inconvenience. A lot of union officials are lazy but sometimes they were genuinely overworked, and a union has limited resources.

I got £2 10s a week on the dole for the first six months, then thirty-eight shillings relief, and my rent was eighteen shillings so it was pretty tight. I learned about all the free stuff you can go to, like RTÉ concerts. I always believed in keeping myself culturally afloat when I was unemployed. I used to go out to my sister's to get fed, so I wasn't starving, but it was hard. I would cook, make vegetable stew and porridge. I wouldn't live out of the chipper or anything.

I also used to rob food. I had a blue bag with a piece of cardboard at the bottom and would go to a big shop in Ballyfermot, hide three or four pounds of sirloin steak under that, and then pay for everything else. I used to rob books with it as well. One time in a record shop I took a Woody Guthrie album and a recording of William Faulkner's Nobel Prize acceptance speech and paid for a record called *It's a Long Way to Tipperary* by the Red Army Choir. I hid the other two behind that one but was stopped by a store detective and asked what I'd bought. I just showed him the Red Army record and he said, 'Oh, that's all right,' and I was free to go. There were two fellas with me who were giving out, saying I was only stopped because it was the Red Army, but when I told them what actually happened, they were mad that I had brought them into such disrepute.

I hardly ever got buses and walked into town from Ballyfermot instead, which is a fair enough distance. I also read a lot – there was very little on the telly and not much on the radio either. I went to Inchicore Library, and into James's Street Library too, to read the papers, where they had a big fire – a godsend. All that reading gave me a distinct advantage in political debate over working people.

I was so engaged in political activity that I focused little on my situation. Had I done so, I would have realized how bleak things were. I had no prospects. I was determined not to go back to England, but I had no money. I was quite poor for a period, and in truth I didn't know what was going to happen to me. There wasn't much prospect of paid work inside the party: Johnny and Mick were about all they could carry.

But I did end up getting a fantastic job in Fiat and the money was great. The company had a pre-delivery inspection plant, doing final checks on fully built-up cars before they go out. It was a small place with maybe sixty to seventy employees down in Grand Canal Street. They were still building the plant on Kylemore Road, and production was carried out in Chapelizod because the place in Wapping Street had burnt down. We wanted maximum employment, so the union wouldn't allow shift work in the car industry or for cars to be brought in fully built up.

Fiat were expanding and bought the next-door block of six or seven small cottages. All the occupants were rehoused, but then the Housing Action Committee occupied the cottages. I had misgivings about this, as did a lot of us, but the homeless families wanted them because they were nice cottages. This wasn't the kind of property speculation we wanted to highlight – this was industrial development. But if your constitution says that homeless families decide what the campaign does, then you have to back them.

They occupied the place and then Kay Security became involved. They had a bit of a name about town as heavies so I went to Cathal Goulding and Seán Dunne. I knew who I was talking to: Goulding was chief of staff of the IRA and I was fairly certain Dunne was with them too. It was a good thing to have a movement like that around. I certainly wouldn't have been able to deal with Kay Security, nor the families, and I wouldn't trust the gardaí to do it. Whatever the IRA did, things eased off after that.

But the publicity around Kay Security embarrassed Fiat, and we used that against them. They contacted us and we met in Sinn Féin headquarters along with the company accountant and the secretary. They agreed to buy the families mobile homes, to make a substantial donation to the DHAC and to sign a document agreeing that there was a housing emergency. It was quite an amicable meeting.

I negotiated with Fiat, never thinking that within a fortnight these people would be interviewing me for a job. That meeting was on a Saturday, and on the Monday I went over to sign the idle book in the union. Danny Browne, an official in the NUVB, told me: 'Do you want a job? There's one in Fiat, starting tonight. Go up to Chapelizod about 9.45 and ask for Mick Holmes.'

I didn't think I stood a chance but off I went to the factory to find Mick. The interview consisted of one question: 'Can you dress an engine?'

'Oh, yeah,' I said.

'OK, start in the underbody.' So I did. I grew the beard as well, further guaranteeing my anonymity.

After a few months there was a strike because they didn't pay us enough for a bank holiday. By law we were supposed to get an average of our bonus for the preceding thirteen weeks. I don't know why we didn't – it was probably more a mistake than a policy. The shop steward from the other shift, John O'Reilly, came down to talk to us. I had looked up the Act and knew the company was wrong, so I helped him, saying that there was no point in the strike because we could win without one. People suggested I go up with John O'Reilly to management. I refused at first, but went in the end. The company secretary didn't say a word. We negotiated and they backed down.

Holmes came up to me. 'I'm after getting threatened with the sack over you! Are you in the Viet Cong or the Chinese Red Army or something? I shouldn't have employed you, you're some kind of a fucking communist!'

'You'll be ok,' I said.

'I'd fucking better be!' he replied. And so I stayed on.

We'd go through twenty-page agreements, which we would scrutinize line by line, examining the meaning of words from every angle. At one meeting, which was supposed to last half an hour, we asked, 'Are we getting paid for the meeting?' When the answer came back that we were, it went on from 9 am to 4.30 pm. People came in and out of the meeting in shifts.

The shop stewards in the factory were George Griffiths and Hughie O'Neill. George Griffiths was a Scouser, a decent man but easily taken off track. You'd send George in to fix up the bonus for Monday and he would come out telling you about the swimming pool we would have in the next factory when they built it. I wanted to be shop steward because I figured out that, once the company knew I was there, it was the best form of protection. I stood against George in the election and beat him by one vote, but he was disgruntled. I couldn't figure out why, because he was no more interested in the work of a shop steward than the man in the moon. But a shop steward got 10 per cent of union dues and that's what he was really annoyed about. I looked up the rule book: the union allowed for cashbook stewards and shop stewards. To consolidate my position, I asked George if he wanted to be the cashbook steward, and of course he was as happy as a pig in shit with that. I campaigned against the introduction of the check-off system, where subs were automatically deducted from wages. I didn't like the idea of collecting money, and I saw a lot of good shop stewards making mistakes, getting union money mixed up with their own. The criticism from the Left was that without it you'd lose contact with the members, but in Fiat I was never out of contact with them.

Hughie O'Neill was more difficult than George. He had boxed for the Golden Gloves. He was a sort of supervisor, close to the company and an extraordinarily dangerous man. One time around 3 am some of us had dozed off – a bit of sleep went on during night shifts – and he threw live mice at us to wake us up. The Italians made him a foreman. He had a following in the factory and was popular, but there was a physical menace about him. He once came on to a moving track, kicked the track and held up a gun. 'You poxes! If I don't get thirty cars off you, that's what you'll get,' he said.

'As long as he's there, you'll never get thirty cars,' I told the production manager.

Mickey Crea once called him a bollocks and O'Neill made a song and dance about it. Everyone spoke like that, of course, including the foremen, but Crea was suspended and a strike was called. The parish priest became involved. The Labour Court was up and running, but it was agreed that we would go to the Catholic Workers' College and that Father Edmund Kent, the head of college, would adjudicate on the dispute.

The company must have primed the priest against me because he started off by saying he had two nephews who were great admirers of Tomás Mac Giolla and Sinn Féin and wanted to do down all the multinationals. When he asked me how I felt about all that, I said, 'Well, it's a very interesting topic but I don't think we're here to deal with that, we're here to deal with this dispute.' Then I asked if I could talk to him privately for a moment in the hall. I took the priest to my class photograph on the wall from the time I went to the college, pointed to it and said, 'You shouldn't believe everything people say.' And I won the case: Mickey was reinstated on full pay.

During a go-slow over bonus payments, O'Neill got hold of John O'Reilly and threatened to hit him. I called a mass meeting. The officials came and I read Hughie the riot act: 'We won't tolerate any kind of violence, and if it carries on we won't work with you. I'll put a picket on the gate until you're sacked, and the Italians will have a decision to make: all of us, or you. Never threaten a shop steward again.' He went apoplectic with rage, foaming at the mouth, effing and blinding, but he sat down in the end. The company moved him sideways and kept him as a foreman. He was put over two fellas in the canteen making tea; anyone else would have been humiliated, but he loved it.

When Hughie's car was blown up it made the front page of the *Evening Herald*. Some people assumed that I had this done through connections with the republican movement, but I wouldn't – it's the wrong way to do things. I felt terrible for him because he told me his wife and family were frightened for their lives. 'Hughie, you have to believe me, I would not do that,' I told him the following morning. He stayed very quiet. Years after, I found out it had been two fellas with drink on them, a piece of stupid drunkenness.

The Italians came in two varieties, social democratic production-minded people or fascists. There were no normal capitalists among them. Italian politics were being played out on the shop floor. The Fiat production manager was called Alberanti. He had been the first person to bring the Fiat apprentices out on strike, when he had been an apprentice himself. When the communist leader Palmiro Togliatti was shot in 1948 there was a huge walkout in Fiat and the Italian Communist Party called a general strike. Alberanti bragged that he insisted on leading out the apprentices: 'The problem is that we measure everything meticulously in this plant: every car, every part, everything we do in the plant we plan. But when it goes out there to the market, there's no plan. That's not my fault, it's your fault. You haven't built the Left in Ireland to make them plan!'

I really liked him, even though he was the enemy. He was a good engineer, competent and pragmatic, not ideologically opposed to the advance of socialism. People who want to pull things down need to think about how to build them up as well.

The NUVB was mainly a craft union in Ireland. Its main base was the vehicle builders in Spa Road in Inchicore (we made all our own buses in Ireland then) as well as a big membership at the loco works in Inchicore and all the assembly workers. There were two sections in the branch: the car workers, who were semi-skilled, and the craftsmen. Each section would only vote on their own issues.

Bonuses were an important part of our payment and caused many arguments. If I negotiate a bonus on the basis of current technology but new technology comes in, which makes a contribution to output, it gets taxed. This payment by results can be seen as tax on new technology that benefits workers. And as new cars came in, there was always a problem about setting the rates and measuring the time. We reached an agreement whereby every job had to be mutually agreed between shop stewards and management. You don't get that kind of language in industrial relations today, but that's what we fought for and got. I was better paid than a car worker in Germany when I started in Fiat.

The night shift was fantastically paid: you would work thirty-two hours and get paid for forty. I would do that one week on and one week off, but the change from days to nights every week gave me an ulcer. I once went to bed at 8 am and was so tired that I woke up, late for work, at 10 pm. But it was a great place to get reading done. I remember John O'Reilly reading *War and Peace* in the toilet! The shift work also made it difficult for me to participate in the Housing Action Committee.

We started to build up solidarity in the branch between the different car plants and formed a relationship with Brittain's, the biggest car plant in the country with 1500 employees. The shop steward was Ted McKenna, a great singer with a fantastic collection of songs who was in the CP for a short period. When Winston Churchill died in 1965, Brittain's gave them a day off but when Roger Casement's remains were being brought home later that year, they asked for a day off and were refused. People took the day anyway, but when they went back to work, they were suspended, so all 1500 walked out. At Fiat we decided to march over the two issues. The slogan at the head of the march was: 'They won't let us bury our patriot dead.'

EIGHT

I was very much into the civil rights argument. As Betty Sinclair put it, if you want to drive a Unionist mad, you don't have to say you want a united Ireland, you just have to say you want equality. They'll intern you and beat you up for it, but that's why you have to keep it up – and you would get allies in Britain. The Communist Party certainly thought we couldn't win the battle against the British in Ireland alone, that we needed friends in the British Labour movement.

The British had a certain affection for the people of Northern Ireland because they had struggled alongside them in the war against the Nazis. It took a lot of work by people like Desmond Greaves and the Connolly Association to overcome that prejudice and educate the British Labour movement about what was happening on the ground in Northern Ireland. I remember hearing Andy Barr speak at the British TUC on the concept of a Bill of Rights in the North; there was huge support for that as the way forward. The British Labour government did very little – Wilson made a speech in 1971 about a united Ireland in fifteen years, but I don't know how serious he was. The only British prime minister who really became involved in Ireland was Blair – he and Gladstone were the only two who ever really thought about it at all.

It's difficult to keep the civil rights movement in harness. The Unionist state was intent on provoking people, bringing in internment and so on, which had a huge negative impact and blew the movement off course. There was a small but important section of the Protestant working class in the trade union movement, which was supportive of civil rights, but everyone went back into their tribes when the state and its naked sectarianism intervened.

The civil rights movement lost its support when the Provos came in. I disagreed with the Provos, but not for the conventional reasons to do with violence. I don't think you can make a rational argument that liberation movements can't use violence. My criticism was not so much that violence would be divisive – in a sense, pushing Britain out of Ireland was always going to be divisive – but that it wasn't going to work. They would say that they were opposed by the violence of the British state and had to defend themselves against it but they went further than defending themselves – they went on the offensive. Paddy Carmody likened it to taking on NATO with a peashooter, and predicted they would end up reforming the Northern Ireland state. The Provos were a product of their time, representing young Catholics in the North who had been brutalized by the state and wanted to bomb their way to Downing Street. They were young and justifiably angry.

The people I condemn are the ones who walked away from the struggle and blamed the trouble on the Northern Ireland nationalists. Those people were to be found in the ranks of the Workers' Party, developing convoluted theories about that situation and half-embracing the two nations theory. The people I knew in the Workers' Party, like Seán Garland or Tomás Mac Giolla, would never have believed there are two nations in Ireland, but created a set of circumstances where that was implicitly what they stood for. I remember being shocked, reading in one of their theoretical magazines how Tony Benn was sectarian to argue for British disengagement and Irish independence. I parted company with them over that. And then they suggested that Catholicism produced an inferior form of capitalism in Ireland than Protestantism, which I thought was quite daft – as though Italian capitalism was always going to be weaker than British capitalism because there were more Protestants in Britain. It was disrespectful to the majority of Irish people because, like it or not, Catholicism has always been the dominant culture.

I worked with republicans in the Housing Action Committee, many of whom had voted for me. They were definitely moving to the left, then tried to become Marxists, giving an inordinate amount of power and influence to people like Eoghan Harris. I once heard Máirín de Búrca say that they were overawed by these people because they had a degree – an unusual view, given that in the Communist Party there was always a genuine relationship between workers and intellectuals. A couple of members had degrees, but people in Ballyfermot didn't go to university. I knew a busman who would often stop the bus off Landen Road and point out the one man from Ballyfermot who had been to Trinity College!

I saw the split in the republican movement along Left–Right lines, but agree with Shakespeare that we should not fall out with traditional republicans who loved their country 'not wisely but too well'. They were not our enemies. And although everyone was pro-official, they were also far too left-wing: if they wanted to be Marxists, all they had to do was join the Communist Party. As republicans they had a wider appeal, and they should have kept the best of that instead of narrowing it down to being an alternative Communist Party.

Some people in the republican movement, like Roy Johnston, had associations with the Communist Party and tried to bring republicans in a certain direction. The Wolfe Tone Society included leftists such as Tony Coughlan, but he was never in the Communist Party. He may have given us money, but people did that without being in the party, including uncles of mine. Desmond Greaves had theories about what the republican movement should do, and my view of the situation in the North was basically his. I'm still involved in the Greaves School and rate him highly. He had a fantastic empathy with the situation and a deep knowledge of Irish history and politics. He made a great contribution, but he was never into taking over the republican movement, only influencing them in his publications. The Communist Party only wanted to get an alliance going between republicans and the Left in the Labour Party – the idea of a takeover is fanciful.

The Provos were wrong in the direction they took, but it was a tactical mistake – in proportional terms the others were much worse. Theirs was an inadequate response to a dreadful situation, encouraging and adding to sectarianism without being sectarian themselves. The responsibility for the condition of Northern Ireland doesn't lie with Gerry Adams or Martin McGuinness: they may have inadequately fought it, but they didn't create it.

The Communist Party in Northern Ireland almost won the right to affiliate to the Northern Ireland Labour Party, which would have had a profound effect and given the labour movement a better chance of taking up the question of civil rights. In the event it didn't, which handed the issue over to others. The trade union movement opted out of serious reform. If there's a case for condemning anyone for the way things developed, it's the failure of the trade union and Labour movement to seriously champion equality for Catholics. They should have done more.

But once push came to shove, the working class divided again. There was a simplistic view that after a couple of heaves against the state the Unionist workers would be able to identify their class enemies and all come over and join us, but I'm afraid that never happened. When certain militants suggested that the answer in Northern Ireland was to arm the workers, I reminded them that many workers *were* armed, but against one another rather than the state.

I believe in James Connolly's view that the national question is fundamentally a social question, so creating equality in Northern Ireland between Catholics and Protestants, Unionists and nationalists, is a first phase of dealing with the national question. If you deprive the Unionists of their so-called privileges or extra rights and make them equal with their fellow citizens, you have a better basis for building common struggles. But while the Unionists have an extra grip within the Northern Ireland state, they will cling onto it for dear life. (I doubt that Unionists – or nationalists – would touch a united Ireland at present, given the debt situation: come and join us and share the €8 billion a year interest we pay to the Germans! A united Ireland inside the euro under German hegemony is far less attractive than the original idea of a united Ireland.)

I was involved in the first stoppage over Bloody Sunday. It was a freezing cold day and we all marched the long road from Fiat in Ballyfermot down to the British embassy. I said we should only stop on the Monday if we stopped on the Wednesday too, when the important demonstration was planned. There was a bit of discussion about that, and then everyone put up their hands to come out on the two days. We all walked out, hundreds of us. Even supervisors wanted to walk out. Alberanti said that anyone could work or not work the next day and no one would be disciplined. You'd expect an employer to say you can demonstrate on your own time, but such was the feeling of shock and horror. Down at the embassy we met thousands of students from Trinity and UCD carrying crosses. There was effectively a general strike that day. It lashed rain, yet the embassy burned.

I knew in my heart that the divisions in the north weren't going to be healed by one isolated incident, but still, there was a temporary shift. The Irish government stopped banging the table and slotted back into the normal groove of relationships with the British. They were afraid and ultimately wanted to defeat the Provos as much as the British did.

I had a tense relationship with the NUVB officials but learned to work alongside full-time officials without letting them dominate me. A weakness of the modern far Left is their inability to become a major influence in the trade union movement. You have to earn trust, and if you make an agreement with somebody you have to keep it. Sometimes you have to break an agreement, but you shouldn't make it a principle.

The NUVB's original intention was to merge with the Amalgamated Engineering Union, but when negotiations broke down we turned to the

TGWU. The idea of a craft union going into a 'labouring' union was difficult to swallow, but they gave the NUVB a more or less autonomous section in the union, so the merger went through in 1972. We were involved in huge battles in the car industry and the ATGWU was able to fund that better than the NUVB would have done. There was a big vote in favour because we got a good deal from them: the percentage was bigger in Dublin than anywhere else in Ireland or Britain, which I think was down to Mattie Merrigan. I was delighted with the merger.

In Ireland the TGWU was always known as the Amalgamated Transport and General Workers' Union (ATGWU), to avoid confusion with the ITGWU. When I joined, the secretary of the Irish region was Norman Kennedy, a right-wing arch-bureaucrat. He had been a member of the Communist Party when he got the job, but it was a very anti-communist union in the late 1940s and communists were banned from holding office at the 1949 conference. When James Larkin 'Jack' Jones campaigned for the job of general secretary, he simply said: 'If you want to ban communists, don't vote for them!'

But people lost their jobs and suffered greatly during this shameful period in the union's history. Arthur Deakin, a vociferous anti-communist and Cold War reactionary, was the man who brought in the ban. Arthur Horner was General Secretary of the National Union of Mineworkers and chairman of the Communist Party. He started his life as a Protestant lay preacher and came to Dublin to join the Citizen Army. On moving to London he took digs in Deakin's house. As secretary of the TGWU, Deakin had a car and a chauffeur, and because he knew Horner, he used to give him a lift to TUC executive meetings. And when Deakin had made a big passionate anti-communist speech, as soon as he finished, he'd walk up to Horner and say, 'Not you, Arthur.' Horner used to tell this story, adding, 'He's not really anti-communist, he's just anti-Russian.' Deakin had a dreadful effect on the union.

The union had been very left wing during the 1930s. Ernie Bevin, the General Secretary, gave money to Spain in 1936 for medical aid during the Civil War. There was a meeting of the Irish region in the Gresham Hotel, with thousands protesting outside giving Christ the King salutes to the delegates going in, but they voted to stick with the union. We lost some members over that. A priest addressed the meeting, then Tommy Geehan from the Revolutionary Workers' Groups – 'the Belfast Robespierre' as he was known – and then a union official. They decided to stay in the union by three votes.

The union had a combative record and the swing to the Right was a big challenge. Bevin, although he was right wing at the end of his life, had gone through left-wing periods. He became part of the British establishment but wasn't an anti-communist like Deakin. At the time there was a paranoia about communists in the union because of the fear of war between the West and the Soviet Union. Churchill had made his famous speech about the iron curtain coming down on Europe, and it certainly came down on the TGWU, who decided to ban communists from office in the union. A man named Henderson, who had lost an arm in the Spanish Civil War, was secretary of the road transport group, about a third of the union, and Arthur Deakin told him he would destroy communism. Henderson replied: 'Hitler just tried that and failed. I don't fancy your chances.' He and other communists lost their jobs in the union, but stayed in as members to try and change it.

By 1957 the ban had been lifted and the communists were the dominant influence on the executive, but back in 1949 – the year the ban came in – Norman Kennedy turned his coat to suit the fashion of the day. Unlike everyone else, I liked Norman and got on well with him. He was right wing but, like most union officials, capable of moving to the Left if it suited him. He was certainly opposed to national wage agreements, but you can be a right-winger and oppose them. Originally a milliner, Kennedy was recruited into the CPNI in Lurgan about 1941 or 42 by Mick McCarthy, who was then in the RAF. The CPNI were big during the war years. Norman used to tell a story about two milliners who came to him and said: 'Mr Kennedy, the boss is not giving us the right rate for the job. He's leaving us a shilling short every week. Would you see what you can do about it?'

'Will I tell him who is making the complaint?' asked Norman.

'Oh, no, don't mention who we are.'

'And if I get the shilling, how will he know what bag to put it in?'

Norman ran the union with a rod of iron, a committee of one. When he lost a vote, he'd say, 'Democracy is about counting heads, not what's in them.' He and Mattie Merrigan had a contested relationship and I would have been on Mattie's side in those battles, but the truth is that I found Norman easier to work with.

During the Loyalist strike in the North in 1974 Len Murray of the British TUC came to Belfast to lead a back-to-work march. Norman, who was fearless and detested sectarianism, marched. He told me about one of the insults thrown at him: 'He called me a Fenian bastard! I'm an Orange bastard, Michael!' He was a Unionist from a Protestant background, but he lived down here because the ATGWU headquarters were based in Dublin from 1922 to 1960.

The ITGWU leader Mickey Mullen once asked me what a republican like me was doing in a British union. 'It's the only place I can talk to working-class Protestants,' I replied. There was sectarianism in the union among members on the two sides and the officers sometimes reflected that. But the ATGWU (now part of Unite) was different to the other British-based unions, which are mostly craft unions, and because we represent people at the bottom of the pile, we always had a big Catholic membership. We built the union on the basis of equality. In the shipyards we had the labourers rather than the craftsmen, so we had more Catholics, and this was reflected in the culture of the union.

Norman's reputation was that he was fair because he treated everyone like a bastard – but he was always very good to me and used to go out of his way to praise speeches I made at the ICTU. 'Let the party influence you, but don't repeat what they say verbatim. Do your own thing,' he told me. Although others saw that as being anti-communist, I took it as well meaning. He was on the verge of retirement and I was in my early twenties, so why would he encourage me?

Jim Larkin Jr and John Conroy are deservedly praised for uniting the Irish trade union movement, but it would never have happened without Norman. He led the biggest union in Northern Ireland and brought the movement there with him. The split in the 1940s was really over the danger of British-based unions having a majority in the leadership of the Irish movement. The existence of two trade union congresses weakened the movement in facing the government. When a single ICTU was being set up it was based on all matters on the island of Ireland being controlled exclusively by trade unionists in Ireland. That's a big deal for Unionists to swallow. There was unanimous support for it as an aspiration, but a fair bit of opposition when it was actually achieved. Andy Holmes said that the TGWU was not afraid to trust its Irish members to deal solely and exclusively with all industrial and political matters affecting the Irish membership. They saw no threat in that to solidarity across the Irish Sea. That still stands – and is at the root of the argument I would later have with Bill Morris.

NINE

Because Ireland had been so shut off during the war years there was a downside to the policy of economic protection. However, this also developed ideals that became very important – our neutrality, for example. Extraordinary events were taking place in Ireland in the 1940s and 50s. Thousands demonstrated in Dublin against Tito for putting the pro-fascist Archbishop Stepinac on trial – and I would venture to say that no other country in Europe, no matter how Catholic, would have been so opposed – but at the same time the Irish were refusing to join NATO, despite Marshall Aid.

Joining the EEC opened things up, but it wasn't necessarily progress. Seán Lemass and Éamon de Valera were initially sceptical about joining, and many people in Fianna Fáil had doubts about the whole concept although they didn't express them publicly. When Vivion de Valera was asked in an interview what way his father had voted, he replied, 'In private.' Lemass made it very clear that joining the EEC would mean defending it, thus saying goodbye to neutrality.

Frank Aiken was easily the most progressive foreign minister we've ever had in Ireland: on disarmament, on championing China's entry into the

UN and on a host of other issues. He showed the role a small country can play even from a nationalist point of view. When they wanted to nobble him, the Americans went to Cardinal Spellman in New York to intervene with de Valera and pull Aiken back from his position on China. Eventually de Valera told Spellman to go and see Aiken himself. He did, and Aiken said something like: 'If St Patrick had been like you, we would never have got the snakes out of Ireland. I believe in confronting your enemies, talking to people and explaining my point of view. China is one of the most populous nations on earth, and we have to bring it in to the UN.' Aiken would start speeches at the UN by saying: 'A lot of people here hate the colonial powers, and I understand that because I personally have fought them.' He had huge credibility with the new African and Arab nations.

What do you do with protectionism in the EEC? This was the question Lemass was asking in the 1950s, when he was in opposition. The capitalists who benefitted from protectionism had no idea of how to grow into wider markets. They were happy behind the protection barriers, doing no developmental work, which drove Lemass mad. He implied that industry is too important to be left to the capitalists. He painted a picture of Ireland beginning to compete on the world stage, the state intervening in industry, picking winners, developing export markets but remaining neutral, much like the Telesis report recommended in 1980. But he abandoned all this when he went into office, partly under the negative influence of the secretary of the Department of Finance, T.K. Whitaker. Whitaker was in that tradition of Irishmen who saw the connection with Britain as progressive. He turned Lemass, sounding the death knell for Fianna Fáil.

Lemass' governing principle was that the British wanted to join the EEC. Edward Heath's government had surveyed the position, realized that their empire was over and considered the EEC a way for Britain to express herself in the world. Opposition to that came from the Labour movement in Britain and whether you could construct British socialism in any meaningful way while in the EEC, which has a unique constitution enshrining competition as being beyond politics. Once you join that club the rules are not up for debate. The bread and butter of normal politics and society is the degree to which the state takes a role, the degree of social welfare and public ownership, but these are all constitutionally prohibited in the EU. You could theoretically elect a communist president in America who could introduce socialism, but electing a communist president of the EU is prohibited by the rules. That informed the debate in Britain.

Nowadays the Conservatives are the primary force against the EU in Britain, championing democracy based on the national state – and the leading force in the Brexit referendum. But you won't find international democracy in the EU. Democracy tends to work best in nation states where people have a common sense of their own communities. The Irish people don't support the idea of being governed by the EU. They welcome it as a set of trade arrangements but don't believe in it as a state.

I remember Michael O'Leary and Tomás Mac Giolla sharing a platform against the Anglo-Irish Free Trade Agreement, and going to meetings run by Sinn Féin in the Bricklayers' Hall. The car workers supported a Dublin Council of Trade Unions demonstration against the agreement in 1964. There was no question of Ireland having a car assembly industry under that, so we were all going to lose our jobs. Sam Nolan spoke (who is still speaking for the Trades Council) and Jack Gannon also represented the Trades Council.

The opposition of the Irish trade union movement to the EEC was influenced hugely by Ruaidhrí Roberts, the General Secretary of Congress. Lemass thought he had nobbled the trade union movement. Study groups went on trips to Europe looking at particular industries, suggesting ways to compete, and Lemass was trying very hard to bring them on board, but the opposite happened. Roberts was quite energized by opposing the EEC.

We lost the referendum very badly. I think people saw joining the EEC as an exciting, modern thing to do. Fianna Fáil were the dominant party, Fine Gael were strongly in favour and it was only Labour that opposed it. The three most important people in the No campaign were Tony Coughlan, Justin Keating and Ruaidhrí Roberts – particularly Keating, because he knew how to work the media better than any other politician. But we were up against huge forces. The Federated Union of Employers and the Confederation of Irish Industry were in favour and Labour and the ICTU were the only serious forces against. We lost, with over 80 per cent voting Yes.

We were building up for a campaign over the EEC. Not only did we demonstrate our opposition, we went on strike and won a protocol attached to the treaties, guaranteeing continuous protection for Ireland's car industry until 1984. If they wanted to get out of car production and bring in assembled cars, the companies would have to create suitable alternative employment. This led to huge conflicts with the Minister for Industry and Commerce, Des O'Malley, who thought he could close down car factories and we would apply for – but not necessarily get – 800 new jobs in Semperit. So we went on strike. We extended free collective bargaining to cover mass boycotts, for example, and not only stopped fully built-up cars coming in to the country, but every nut and bolt. These were drawn-out battles, resulting in more favourable results.

I used to be up and down to Brittain discussing negotiations and so on but when it came to the EEC we all had a common interest, whichever company we worked for. Once, during a dispute in Brittain, there was a bit of a row on the picket line where somebody was knocked to the ground by gardaí. I stopped the work at Fiat and we all marched up to Brittain on the Long Mile Road. It looked like a scene from a film, hundreds of workers on the march to support their colleagues on the picket line.

Brittain was losing the market and began building Japanese as well as British Leyland cars, but that was never going to be acceptable to Leyland. We organized a strike and effectively prevented everything from Leyland coming in for months, including cars, buses and farm machinery. Although we triumphed with the strike, when we went back to work there was very little of the market left. We had to share shifts, with people doing two days, two days and one day, and although work built up again it was bleak to begin with and didn't feel like a victory. A strike is an awful blunt instrument, to be used as a weapon of last resort.

The car industry was protected under the protocol we won on entering the EEC. Whatever proportion of the market a company had, that's how many cars they had to produce every year. When they reached that number they could import cars, but this meant smaller companies could import more cars than bigger ones. To keep afloat, Brittain did a deal to make Japanese cars.

I became shop steward in Fiat and chair of the branch. The chair is supposed to attend most negotiations but I didn't because the officials disliked me. I was working in the union office while an official was on holiday and Brittain said they wouldn't have me as a negotiator because I was working for a competitor. The shop stewards decided that we don't allow management to dictate who negotiates for us. We issued strike notice. As soon as we did, they told us they had lost the Japanese work and were closing. One of the shop stewards told me, 'You have to fall on your sword, Brother O'Reilly. We're not going on strike.' We had to do a soft-shoe shuffle out of that.

We argued, before we joined the EEC, that the protection de Valera had brought in was the worst form. We said that employers should be allowed greater access to the market in proportion to the amount of components they made for the cars in Ireland. We wanted to use and export the country's zinc and lead. Keating was hugely enthused over that but didn't do anything about it as a minister and so today all these cars are brought in and they're no cheaper. People were told that car workers would lose their jobs but that cars would be a dime a dozen. This never happened. I'm not in favour of cars being cheap because of the environmental concerns, but that's what people were told.

In 1974 an occupation of Reg Armstrong's and McKearn's Motors took place. There were maybe eighty or ninety workers in Armstrong's, but only ten or so turned up to occupy the plant. One of the workers, Bertie Galbraith, composed a song to the tune of a Nelson Eddy song, which began: 'March, march, march, the men of Armstrong!' He sang it on the walk to the plant and I had to bite my tongue to keep from laughing. Just before the bridge to Ringsend the workers hesitated. Albert McCready, being older and fitter than me, was given the job of jumping over the wall and chopping the lock off the back door with a hatchet. I kicked in the door to the boardroom and said to the workers: 'This is your boardroom now, we're taking this place over. We're also blocking all the cars. We have pickets on the docks and all the dockers are supporting us.' We produced a calendar, which we sold. The compromise in the end was that we got Packard Electric out of it and they had first right to the jobs there, but it wasn't a place we were mad about. The rates were good for that particular industry but we kept a blockade on fully built-up cars until the fellas were given enhanced redundancy terms.

A case was taken out against the union. The McWilliams judgment was issued against us (essentially a tort against the union, as if the 1906 Trade Disputes Act never existed). The only person with a copy was Pat Sweeney, an RTÉ industrial relations correspondent, who took it down in shorthand. We were liable for all costs to inconvenienced customers. Mattie Merrigan was threatened with jail and the ESB workers said they would call a strike over that. Comrade Charles Haughey intervened and gave all the workers in Chrysler jobs as caretakers in the civil service as well as a top-up in wages equal to what they would have earned as car workers. Every week those caretakers had an hour off, when they would leave their government departments and go down to our office where a fella would come on a motorbike with brown envelopes for all of them – incredibly, this really happened

Barry Desmond condemned it as populism and read the whole agreement into the Dáil record. It was denounced by Labour as something immoral, a complete affront to social democracy. I think Haughey was right: he made that choice rather than let Mattie go to jail and the ESB go on strike and it was a terrific victory for trade union power. We stood by the members: we didn't keep the car industry intact, but we looked after them until the end of their days, and that is an achievement. It's important that shop stewards and young trade unionists learn that you can defy situations and win.

Nobody ever complained that these strikes were political and I was always asked, 'Why isn't everybody else doing it?' Workers in other protected industries were facing job losses but lacked the advanced level of consciousness of car workers. Most of the car workers would have voted for Fianna Fáil or Labour: they weren't revolutionaries but were prepared to take off their coat and fight for their jobs.

Some people thought we should put all our energies into getting redundancy but I explained that we would never, ever ask for redundancy. Even if the terms went up and up and up, we would still say no. There might come a time when we would have to settle as a safety net, but we had to maintain the fight for their jobs. I wanted a better industrial settlement with suitable alternative jobs and we got a combination of both. It shows the limits of trade unionism – at the end of the day we had no party to politically express what we wanted.

Tony Coughlan campaigned vigorously against the euro, seeing it as emasculating the capacity of an Irish democracy to function. He was right, and the mess we're in is partly a result of being in the euro. Democracy as we understand it is based on national constructs. There's no international polity. The Irish people accept that wealth should be distributed from Dublin to Kerry, even if we don't always agree how that should be done. But that doesn't happen at an international level: wealth shouldn't be distributed from Germany to Ireland. People in Europe are being told that they can vote for whoever they want but that they can't change policies, which are technocratically determined by law and treaties.

Some in the Left want to change Europe as a whole, while others want to revert to national democracies. At the moment I tend towards the more national approach, keeping European solidarity going while finding allies where we can but developing our own economy, which is still quite underdeveloped. I would prefer us to float our currency and take our chances. I don't want to see us having less democratic control over our economy. We'll end up out of the euro, not by our own decision but simply because we won't be able to stay in. We are the only country in the EU whose major export partners are not in the euro, and these contradictions will out in the end. It's going to be the dominant issue of the twenty-first century and it will be determined by whether there are left-wing governments elsewhere in Europe.

TEN

The Communist Party of Ireland was originally established in 1921 by Roddy Connolly and fought on the republican side in the civil war. The IRA rank and file in the 1920s were quite open to being influenced by the communists – this was before Stalin started his disastrous policy of attacking religious believers, which drew the Catholic Church down on them. Some of the responsibility, however, lies at the door of the communists: they were right to deny the Church influence on the state, but they did more than that, persecuting people for their religious views even though Lenin had left copious writings denouncing the practice. As a result, you couldn't mention socialism without being drawn into a discussion of religion and the existence of God. This original organization was disbanded in 1923, with the Revolutionary Workers' Groups being set up in 1930.

In 1933 another party – the Communist Party of Ireland (CPI) – emerged out of the Revolutionary Workers' Groups, based more on the orthodox communism of the time. At first the new party opposed the Second World War that had just broken out in 1939, claiming it was simply a clash of two imperialist camps. Members in the North then supported the British war effort when the Soviet Union was invaded in 1941, swelling numbers as a result.

In the South the CPI entered the Labour Party, forming a branch in Dublin that became the party engine; many were expelled after the war in a big red scare. Michael O'Riordan spoke against antisemitism at a meeting in Cork. Afterwards Gerald Goldberg, a local businessman, gave him a fiver. Mick O'Riordan put it into the Labour Party funds and was promptly suspended for taking money from a Jew. He subsequently formed the Cork Socialist Party, getting a bigger vote than Tom Barry, the war of independence hero, in a by-election. In 1947 the communists formed the Irish Workers' League, which went on to become the Irish Workers' Party, which I joined. It bears no relation to the later Workers' Party.

We brought about the reunification of the Communist Party during the Troubles in the North. I never agreed with the idea of two communist parties. Their programmes were identical, but the title of the Irish Workers' Party programme was 'Ireland her Own', while the CPNI programme's title was 'Ireland's Path to Socialism'. It was socialism for Protestants and national freedom for the Catholics. This was inevitable but not unprincipled. If you want to have an impact in Northern Ireland you have to put much more emphasis on socialism than nationalism; you are forced to couch your propaganda in those terms. Proletarian Belfast, with its tens of thousands working in the shipyards, dictated it. The word socialism was more acceptable in the North partly because the British Labour Party spoke about it, whereas in the South socialism would speak more in terms of progressive national development.

I was on the joint council of the two communist parties and was involved in negotiating the joint programme. The merger was straightforward. Mick started his speech at the huge unification conference: 'In a few days' time you will wake up and hear a song called "It's a Great Day for the Irish". But 15 March 1970 is a great day for the Irish because we're putting the Communist Party together.'

The party's industrial committee used to meet in Castlebellingham with Special Branch in attendance, who were invariably the only other people in the hotel. We'd meet under the name of the Leinster Chess Club, otherwise we wouldn't have been given the room, although I think the hotel had an idea who we were. I certainly didn't look like a chess player.

I was on the executive of the CPI. We didn't deal with the North that differently to how we did when there were two parties. There was a certain amount of natural autonomy when dealing with particular issues. Once decisions are made, you have to go out and make them happen on the shop floor.

But the committee meetings were endless. I'm always struck by Walter Lippmann's remark: 'If communism ever comes to America, get on a committee, it's where everything happens.' The Left is notorious for committees for everything. The Italian communist Luigi Longo made a great speech when Enrico Berlinguer became General Secretary of the Communist Party in 1972:

> This is a great moment for our party, the first time there has been unanimous support for a young man who was never in the partisan army, never laboured in the fields, never led a strike, who is middle-class, and whose wife and family are staunch Catholics. He never wrote a theoretical article, so how does he have the talent to take over as General Secretary? He possesses a great thing for a communist to have: he has an iron arse.

Berlinguer was a very able leader, but it's true – if you can sit interminably at committee meetings, you'll make it on the Left some day.

Party members were given holidays to eastern Europe. I took advice from Paddy Carmody, though: 'Never go; it may become part of your lifestyle. Never get that dependent.' I did go to the Soviet Union for two weeks in January 1970, but that was on a political delegation. The CYM was invited after the invasion of Czechoslovakia and I wanted to be there because I was worried about who else might have gone and what they might have signed or said there.

While in the Soviet Union we also visited Georgia, where I had a funny experience. The sole came off one of my boots and I asked a doorman at our accommodation where I could get someone to mend them. He happened to have a cobbler's shop, a little workshop with a last and a huge photograph of Stalin on the wall. 'There may be a thaw in Moscow, but as long as Georgia is there Stalin will have some admirers,' I thought to myself. Anyway, he fixed my shoes.

The interpreter laughed when I told him about this. 'I bet that wasn't in the Five Year Plan!' I said, but I was making a point: how do you anticipate, say, for how many times a car is going to break down? You have to stay flexible. They couldn't plan for the sole coming off my boot and could have said, 'Comrade, that's not in the plan, so you'll have to walk around on one foot.' But instead they innovated.

I met the head honcho – or deputy head honcho – of the Leningrad Young Communist League and asked him through an interpreter, 'What theoretical problems have been created by the Soviet intervention in Czechoslovakia in relation to national self-determination, democracy and communist parties finding their own road?' He gave me a most wonderful answer: 'None.' That's the Soviet Union for you!

We met mostly apparatchiks on that trip. Many weren't even communists, just people who might have been managers in Dunnes Stores and been promoted, it seems. Not all of them, though: our interpreter, for example, had read all of Solzhenitsyn's works, more than I had. I asked him if that stuff wasn't banned and he said, 'Yeah, but that's just for the masses. In the party, we read nothing else but banned books.' I realized there was an inner life in the party, that these were intelligent people who were up to speed with things in the West.

I tried to arrange to meet Neil Goold, an Irish communist living in the Soviet Union, even though Johnny Nolan had discouraged me from doing so. One of the interpreters said, 'You want to meet the Irish Chinaman?' Goold was obviously still pro-Stalin, like the Maoists. I never did get to meet him. People who knew him gave the impression that he was a bit eccentric but a great communicator. When he was interned in the Curragh during the Second World War the bishops campaigned to get him out because the right-wing republicans said he was converting them to communism. He gave the Party a house on 37 Pembroke Road for their offices, while he himself was living out of condensed milk cans and sleeping on people's floors.

Anastas Mikoyan, who had been high up in the Politburo, gave a speech about Lenin on the centenary of his birth. He was like a ripe fig, small and dark and full of wrinkles. It wasn't a great speech but this fella was with Stalin in Baku in 1912 producing leaflets for oil workers in a dozen languages and he was still there in 1970. You got an idea of his strength of character, that Bolshevik certitude, which, of course, can be a bad thing when you're in power.

In Leningrad on a victory parade I really got a sense of what the Second World War meant to these people. I made a bollocks of myself with a stupid comment about some war photographs on display. Just to make conversation, I said to one of our guides, 'Of course, the cold had a big impact on the Germans.'

The man looked at me and said, 'You see all these German bodies? There are holes in them. It's not the weather that put them there, it's the Red Army!' I wanted the ground to open up and swallow me.

Mick gave me money to buy my interpreter a bottle of whiskey and some cigarettes. 'Of course, you know the Soviet Union will never make you socialist,' he said, which is a big mouthful coming from him. Nor would it. The automated lifts in the hotel still had three attendants watching them. Hundreds of people were sweeping the snow. Some aspects of life were impressive. The education system was very good, the level of literacy, of reproduced culture among the masses. Everyone read ferociously: Tolstoy, Gorky, Dickens, and could discuss literature, but not modern, cutting-edge stuff: it was backward in terms of contemporary culture.

I was there in a time of thaw since Khrushchev. Brezhnev was just a big wet blanket, who wasn't for anything or against anything. He went in every morning and got his eight hours done. There was no ideological edge to the place at all. I wouldn't say it was like that in Stalin's time, when there would have been some kind of Marxist edge to things, even a distorted one. Eric Hobsbawm went to the Soviet Union once and said most of the people he met wouldn't even be let into the British Labour Party.

It's one thing to support the Soviet Union but it's another to support everything the Soviet Union ever did. There was a big controversy in the party over a book by two Jewish writers who wanted to leave the Soviet Union and go to Israel. I argued that if people wanted to go to Israel, they should go. The Soviet Union was supporting the Arab world and Israel was a counter-revolutionary state, but you don't advance a cause by making people live in a state when they don't want to. Cuba had the right attitude: 'If you don't want to help us build the revolution, fuck off.'

Mick was already working on undermining the Czech business. With the exception of Betty Sinclair, the leading members in the North were all with us over Czechoslovakia. But what do you do when you've condemned the event? When the Czechs write to you and say, 'Comrade, we'd like you to come here on holiday and talk about the future,' do you say no?

Perhaps we were more liberal in the South. I got the impression that they were actually more open to Eurocommunism in the North, but everything became polarized into pro-Czechoslovakia or pro-Soviet, a real communist or a revisionist. Proper debate diminished, as it always does with factions in socialist movements. Following the Soviet line became a slavish process with very little criticism allowed.

It's hard to see how this attitude would work in the trade union movement, although it did in some ways. Andy Barr had originally opposed the intervention in Czechoslovakia and I remember people saying he was soft because he didn't resign his membership of various state committees when internment was introduced in the North in 1971. It was suggested that, as a trade unionist in a car factory, I should make a speech taking him on. I didn't come down in the last shower, so I said to them, 'Well, how come you won't do it?' I actually liked Andy Barr and thought he was a great trade union leader and a courageous man. Perhaps people were afraid of him. Being the sole communist on the executive of the ICTU was not easy for Andy.

I was invited onto a committee developing the Telesis report in order to give input from the Left. The report explored the creation of large industries with an indigenous base, leading to huge markets through collaboration between state and private sector. I approved of this sort of development because, as well as moving towards socialism, it created a better base in the country.

Mick ran in a local election during the time I wasn't working, so I would spend the whole day with him sometimes, printing leaflets, canvassing with him at night. He was trying to work me round to his position, to see the Soviet Union differently. He would talk about Lenin and revisionism, asking me if I had read Lenin's *'Left-Wing' Communism*.

One night I became annoyed with him as we were walking home down Marrowbone Lane because he had been at me like white noise all day, so I said, 'I'll tell you what we'll do. Write a manifesto and we'll bring it up there to the flats, saying that you were a bricklayer on the Berlin Wall and a tank driver in Hungary. See how well that goes down.' I thought he might hit me and stepped off the path to make myself smaller – Mick would never hit anybody smaller than him – and we walked amicably down to the end of the street. Because I had no money he would always buy me four pints and give me my bus fare – this time, however, when we got to St Catherine's Church he just said goodnight and left me to walk home to Ballyfermot. The next day we carried on as normal – the incident was never mentioned again.

In 1975 the Russians sent the head of their trade union congress, Alexander Shelepin, former head of the KGB, on a visit to Britain. There was an outcry. You can't put in a fella like that to run the unions: it would be like the British putting an army general in charge of the TUC. I had a stand-up row with Mick O'Riordan and Noel Harris. What brought things to a head was a document in 1975, which had the effect of retrospectively reversing what we said over Czechoslovakia. Communists make policy based on a fundamental political statement with an assessment of the world and Irish situation, analysis of the balance of forces, a set of aims and objectives. Mick changed our position on Czechoslovakia.

I said to Mick: 'Why don't we go back to the French revolution and have a split over that? Maybe I agree with Danton and you agree with Robespierre.' You should be able to live with contested ideas in a big organization and not feel as if they are insinuating themselves into every other issue. It's a Stalinist mode of thought, like the argument with the Chinese: the Communist Party of Ireland had more of an emphasis on China as a negative force in the world than on America, which I thought was extraordinary. Not because I was particularly keen on all the things China was doing, but if there was a bad wolf in the world it was American imperialism. China came a poor second.

Mick attacked Joe Deasy during a pre-conference meeting. There had been a demonstration in Dublin during the Czech events in 1968 against the Russian invasion of Czechoslovakia, the Americans in Vietnam and the British in Northern Ireland, all under one banner. Roy Johnston was involved, people on the left of Labour, Trotskyists, republicans – it was a smallish demonstration of a couple of hundred. Joe Deasy marched and Mick went spare. I didn't march because I thought the equation was wrong: I didn't quite see the Russians as imperialists like the Americans in Vietnam or the British here. Their intervention was more about keeping the internal structure of the Soviet Union intact than anything in Czechoslovakia itself.

I wasn't a delegate to the conference, even though I owned the branch premises – a wooden shed in my garden with a big sign that read 'Communist Party, Ballyfermot Branch'. Packie Early and I put it up. They'd plug the light into my house and even after I left the party they would ask to use my electricity during their meetings!

The branch comprised about fifteen or twenty regular members. We were active in tenants' and community organizations, sold the paper around the pubs and produced leaflets on local issues. Oddly enough, we never had any problems from the Church over that. But I wasn't a great activist in the local branch because the union took up most of my time. I didn't get one vote when conference delegates were elected, which was quite something as I had been on the executive, and shows how bad the split was. On Monday night I'd have the political committee, on Tuesday night a union meeting, on Wednesday night a lecture, Thursday night off, but Friday night selling the paper, to say nothing of meetings at the weekend in Belfast or elsewhere – how do you fit in the life of a branch on top of that? It was hectic and I was also working five days a week in a car factory.

We left the party in the mid-1970s over its slavish following of the Soviet Union. A Communist Party is not like a labour party and democratic centralism has features that are easily corruptible. Once you gain control of a democratic centralist organization your opponents usually go down the plughole. Paddy Carmody was removed as editor of the paper after fifteen or twenty years of doing an excellent job. It was humiliating for him and ultimately there was nothing left for us.

Leaving the party created better working relationships with the members still in it and the first thing we did was to set up the Irish Marxist Society. We ran lectures and produced a theoretical journal. Anthony Cronin spoke on Marxism and literature, Paddy Devlin on sectarianism, Naomi Wayne on women's liberation, Andy Boyd on trade unionism. But all that was like being in the Communist Party again. The committee met on a Monday, we produced a bulletin and circulated it, ran lectures, printed a journal: what was the difference?

Immediately after our departure, Paddy quoted a slogan from Marx: 'Communists do not stand apart from the Labour movement.' That immediately justified entry into the Labour Party, having argued the opposite for decades: we were still communists, but we weren't separate, and in and of the Labour movement. Most people joined the Labour Party. I only did so later. I was becoming engulfed in the trade union movement, which was occupying more and more of my time. Leaving the party didn't make that make much difference to me in terms of trade union work and within a year I was working in Dundalk.

Eurocommunism was an attempt to develop a viable independent communist strategy for western Europe, based on pluralist democracy. I don't think we would have called ourselves Eurocommunists, but that's where our politics were coming from. We would have seen ourselves as mainstream communists. A lot of people, such as young Jim Larkin and Justin Keating, took the party with them.

I left the Communist Party because I felt my communism was being tainted. Had I stayed it would have meant compromising deeply held ideals. It was a hard thing to do. I didn't half believe in communism, I fully believed in it.

ELEVEN

… the British government has no right in Ireland, never had any right in Ireland, and never can have any right in Ireland …

James Connolly

I remember, as a sixteen-year-old, looking up at an official speaking at a union meeting and thinking, as Yosser Hughes later said in *Boys from the Blackstuff*, 'I could do that.' I liked the idea of being a union official. I also wanted to follow Mattie Merrigan. I thought I could make a difference and that other officials wouldn't carry out his legacy with my level of loyalty, even though he was a Trot and I was supposed to be a Stalinist – and it's usually the other way round, the older man a communist and the younger a Trotskyist. It never affected our friendship. I loved Mattie. He helped me in the union in a hundred and one ways. We met every Saturday night for over thirty years, when we would dissect the week in the pub.

The car industry was a bolshie place and I didn't always get on with the officials. I was involved in a branch of the union known as the Politburo, which most of the officials disliked because it insisted on performance and accountability. Sometimes workers themselves are afraid to exercise responsibility, or don't even think that they should, that it should rest with a paid official. We did not take that view: our wages and conditions were of paramount importance to us, more important than the ego of an official. If we had to fight with these people, we fought and we usually won.

I applied for, and got, a job in Dundalk, taking over from Raymond Waters, who had been the official for thirty-seven years and twice mayor of Dundalk. Raymond was a tough, deeply religious man, an ex-boxer with cauliflower ears and a great sense of fighting injustice. He stayed on a bit longer than he was being paid for in order to help me find my feet, but did not interfere. Mattie once told him, 'This is difficult, Raymond, but he's in the hot seat now. If he asks you for advice, help him, but if he doesn't, let him make his own mistakes.'

The first night I walked into the branch Raymond tugged my shoulder and whispered, 'Don't say anything about the prayer.' And lo and behold, at the start of the meeting they all stood up to say the ecumenical prayer recited in Dáil Éireann. I didn't want to start on a bad note but at the end of the meeting I said, 'I don't think branches of the Transport Union are a place for prayers. I don't want to be offensive to anybody, but we can't do this.'

One member said: 'I hope you're not going to force a vote on this, on your first night in Dundalk. It'll be all over the town.' I said I didn't want a vote; I was only making a suggestion that we examine it. They asked me to leave the room and when I came back in, they said: 'Raymond is retiring in December. We'll say the prayer at the next two meetings of the branch. A lot of us will be leaving along with him, and there'll be new elections. The incoming branch committee can discuss the prayer, and it can be decided at an AGM.' And that was it. We abolished the prayer in January.

The next day I rang Mattie to complain about the prayer. 'Get down off the ceiling and relax. You'll come across far bigger difficulties than that in your life,' he said. I told him I wasn't having any of it. He replied: 'OK, you're the man up there, you do what you want to do. But tell me, are the prayers working for them? Are they getting any extra increases?' I banged the phone down on him and then burst out laughing. It was silly to get worked up about something so trivial, what with all the other injustices in the world.

Working in the car industry turned out to be a cause as well as a job. It was right where the Communist Party's analysis was in terms of what would happen to protected industries, the effect of the EEC and imperialism, and I was able to lead campaigns and political strikes on those issues, perpetual class warfare at the point of production. But when I left the car industry, in some ways I joined the trade union movement ragtag and bobtail, with all kinds of workers. I was looking after dockers and drivers and clerical workers and local authority workers and skilled engineers and more besides. The branch was a microcosm of the whole trade union movement. There were ninety different sections and about 3000 workers in the Dundalk ATGWU. We were bigger than the ITGWU in the town, and we went out as far as Clones and Greenore and even had a few members in Newry. It was an introduction to the whole wider trade union movement.

What struck me first was the sheer loneliness. As a convenor I was always surrounded by ten or twelve shop stewards every day, dealing with problems in the factory. In Dundalk I'd sit in the office and nobody would phone up – that didn't last long, though, because once people got used to me they never stopped phoning. But I got into the rhythm of the place, working with people and developing great relationships with shop stewards.

I was no longer as involved in politics. Instead I concentrated on industrial relations, dealing with almost every industry under the sun. Getting settlements for that many workplaces is difficult. You can't do them all at the same time – the strongest sections go first. It's hard work, and the employers on the other side of the table know exactly what you're trying to do.

Moving to Dundalk was a big sacrifice for Mary. It meant buying a house and leaving family and friends, but we ended up making a great success of it and really enjoyed our time there – my first challenge, within days of arriving, was talk of a tax strike. The ITGWU called a tax demonstration on the Sunday to counteract a strike on the Thursday, which is what the

Trades Council wanted. I supported the Thursday strike but was taking my life in my hands because I hadn't the faintest idea what the response would be. The shop stewards rose to it like lions and organized a huge demonstration. It was addressed by a speaker from Congress, who were half in and half out of the campaign. They didn't want direct confrontation with the government, but when they saw the numbers, they were determined to lead it. That Sunday three senior officers of the ITGWU came down for their demonstration, which was attended by two and a half people and a dog. The Trades Council action, on the other hand, was a huge success.

A million people attended the tax march in Dublin. Paddy Carmody, secretary of Dublin Trades Council, who called the strike, died of a heart attack the day before. I remember walking out of the house and collapsing, weeping at the news of his sudden death. They say someone's not dead as long as you remember them and he'll always be a big feature of my life. Paddy was a great mind, a great thinker and a great character altogether. He had a big head, like Karl Marx, with a big brain, and a capacity to enliven a situation with a different perspective.

It was the biggest demonstration in the history of the city, but brought about tax cuts rather than tax reform. The Progressive Democrats were skilful in enabling this agenda because we didn't have a sufficiently socialist culture to exploit. It could have gone the other way, channelled in the direction of tax equity.

Mattie told me about the two breweries in Dundalk, the old Macardle's, and Harp Lager, built in the early 1960s. They were across the road from each other but, he said,

> Those two breweries are as different as chalk and cheese. In Macardle's you'll find paternalism and hospitality, an easy style of negotiation, and a bit of reverence towards the employer. In Harp you'll find nothing but antagonism to everything. The building of Harp coincided with the rationalization of the docks. We got loads of our docker members into Harp Lager, and they brought the docks with them.

And never a truer word was spoken. The difference between the styles of negotiation on one side of the road to the other was unbelievable. One was fifteen rounds of brutal fighting, and the other was very gentlemanly and courteous. The workers were different too. Mattie's suss on the place was absolutely spot-on.

S&S Corrugated was a large company based in Dundalk. The administrative arm was in the US but all the manufacturing was done in Ireland. They had relocated in Ireland after the Great Northern Railway closed in 1958 because of the skilled local engineering workers. The corrugated paper machines they made took three years from the time they were ordered until they were finished. National wage agreements at that time lasted two years, so the three-year cycle gave us a chance to get into some free collective bargaining with them.

Instead of negotiating with the company itself we dealt with Marty Ellenberg, who came over from New York. He'd stay in Dundalk for a month or more and always bought Harris tweed suits when he was here. He was the most suave, sophisticated and brilliant negotiator I have ever met. He had a basket of European currencies, measuring the Irish punt against them over three years, but of course that didn't make any difference to me in dealing with the cost of living in Dundalk.

When inflation hit around 22 per cent a year, we negotiated an unprecedented 47 per cent increase over three years, done so that the big money came in the last year. That gave the company a chance to grow its markets and also gave our members good money at the end. I thought I had done a great job and I went down to give my recommendation in a wonderful speech, but as often happens in the Labour movement, it was rejected – narrowly enough, but it was still a rejection.

'Well, our members have rejected this,' I said to Marty. 'As Oliver Twist said in relation to the porridge, "I want more." I have no brilliant insight as to where you're going to get it from, but you're just going to have to give us more. When they say no, they say no and that's it. I'm standing over their decision.'

'Mick, you've got nothing to apologize for,' he replied. 'You know what we should do? Just get in the ring and do fifteen rounds with one another.' He opened his coat. 'The trouble is, if you lay a glove on me, I'll drop dead. I've got a bad ticker – this place is fucked. I gave you too much. What do you want to do?'

'I think we should call a doctor and test what you've said to me – get in somebody from outside.'

We brought in Professor John Lynch from the Irish Productivity Centre and Brendan Revell from Fóir Teoranta, the state bank for rescuing companies in trouble, who I knew when he was running Jaguar Rover Triumph cars. The essence of their report was that we actually got too much, which is a compliment, really.

Then I said to Ellenberg: 'You're holding all the cards now. I won't be recommending a strike over this, but they may choose to fight. Maybe you can humiliate them and make them accept this, but you won't get the work off them. They'll be sullen and destroyed. Give us another 1 per cent or something.' And he agreed, and gave us a little bit extra. Had the workers voted to go on strike, I would have pleaded with them not to. A strike is a big deal.

In fact the deal sailed through, but the place closed down seven or eight years later and when the parent company in New York went into receivership they decided to sell the patents. John Bruton had just become minister of finance and was wailing about public expenditure. I asked him to put in a bid for the patents. It wouldn't have cost much, but I might as well have been talking to the wall. 'Government shouldn't do things like that,' was his point. I told him it wouldn't even interfere with competition, because no one else in Ireland was making corrugated sheets. I tried to get companies who used a lot of packaging to put a consortium together to bid, but Bruton wouldn't help at all.

Bruton was going through a real Thatcherite period, and we were interrupting his train of ideological thought with our pragmatic idea, which might have saved a few hundred jobs. He was adamant, though, and after that I decided that opposition was the only place for Fine Gael. I've no evidence that Fianna Fáil would have done something, but I do have a suspicion that had we gone to Haughey, he would have sent someone over on spec and put in a bid for the right price.

We were well paid in Fiat. I was getting £110 a week when I left in 1978; the average wage then would have been around £60. As an official I got £10 a week less to make sure I didn't become part of a privileged bureaucracy! Jack Jones didn't believe in paying officials well – including himself – he took the ethos of the Spanish Civil War into the union with him. There was great spirit in the union and it was a rewarding job. I was already involved in the leadership, on the executive of the ATGWU and determining policy. I wasn't an oppositionist shop steward, although I had my moments of opposition to certain officials.

I like to think I ran the union from a rank-and-file perspective, never making decisions over the heads of workers. This wasn't born out of altruism, but rather out of convenience: if they know what the problem is they can be part of bringing about a solution. Mattie told me once: 'If they know you're on their side, you'll be all right. They won't throw garlands at you, but they'll trust you. If they mistrust you, you're fucked.'

It's essential that younger officials develop confidence in themselves and are open to their shop stewards. I run shop stewards' courses in the union and tell them: 'I'm going to describe a problem, and on the day you have this problem the phone is broken, the union official can't be contacted, you can't get through to head office and you have to think your way through it – with nobody else to help you.' You have to take responsibility if you're going to build a movement. And if you can't negotiate a wage agreement, if you can't create a culture that can manage wages and conditions of workers in an advanced way, you're never going to run a country.

I remember convincing shop stewards in Harp that during a period of high taxation and mass unemployment we shouldn't look for a wage increase but for shorter hours. Imagine this happening on a huge scale; the ICTU saying that, because of mass unemployment, we are going to ban overtime and have disputes over shorter hours to eat into unemployment.

This engenders a process of thinking as a movement of an alternative way of running the world, a different set of values, which creates a different consciousness. Larkin's great idea was that socialism doesn't advance based on its own internal logic and reason but on the needs of the hour. You have to take the theory and bring it down to earth, to the immediate needs of ordinary people, and they have to move the thing forward.

There was a large engineering works called Echo, making small parts for computers, with a mainly female workforce. Mattie Merrigan had put in huge amounts of work and achieved almost equal pay, with the women now up to what was called the male janitor's rate – the lowest-paid male rate: this meant a roughly 40 per cent increase for thousands of women, over which the company threatened to close. I took over and did a deal with the company that won them the equal rate. In the process, however, thirteen male workers left the union because I wouldn't take action to restore their differential. I told them that there was no skill difference between them and the women and the company had been robbing the women for years. The men left and were poached by the ITGWU.

I met Mickey Mullen, the ITGWU General Secretary – one of the few meetings I had with him because he died shortly afterwards – and we went through a long list of members we were supposed to have robbed off each other. When we came to these thirteen, Mullen jumped in before I even opened my mouth, and said: 'We were wrong. We shouldn't have done it, and it was just some eejit of a local official.'

A 1947 document signed by Gilbert Lynch of the ATGWU and William McMullen of the ITGWU stipulated that there would be no more poaching in P.J. Carroll's tobacco factory: the ATGWU would get all the women and the ITGWU all the men. I was amazed. Mattie explained that the ITGWU had been happy with it at the time because women, on half pay, paid lower union contributions – but they'd never anticipated women getting equal pay. 'We're ahead at the races now. Leave it there,' he said.

Mattie was vice president of the ICTU at a time when a lot of anti-smoking campaigns were taking off. Of course, people who worked in Carroll's thought that everybody should smoke – even that it should be compulsory. The government had hammered cigarettes in that year's budget. Mattie did a broadcast about the budget, but never said a word about the increase on cigarettes. Local ITGWU members had canvassed the women in Carroll's to give out to Mattie over this and leave the union.

He arrived to speak to hundreds of women in the canteen, took off his trilby hat, put it down on the table and said: 'I understand you're all very angry that I didn't give out about the taxation of cigarettes. How many of you would make your children smoke to keep yourselves employed if you thought it would make them sick?' To a stunned silence, he picked up his hat, put it on and walked out. Game, set and match. It was the best sentence I ever heard at a meeting and the issue was never raised again during my time in Dundalk.

One morning, as I was catching up on my correspondence – I used to come in early but not tell anyone – I opened a letter from Mattie. It was 1979, shortly before the papal visit. There had already been a row in the union because a group of atheists and freethinkers wanted to protest against certain aspects of the visit, including the fact that the ITGWU had produced their own gift for the Pope. Mattie gave this group the union's hall in Dublin for a meeting, and some of the officers in the union thought I could get Mattie to withdraw the use of the hall. I told them they could raise it with him themselves if they wanted to. At that time, people had 'floating days'; besides the general holidays, an individual could choose to take a day or two off here and there for whatever reason, even though the factory would still be open. Dealing pragmatically with the practicalities of the papal visit, the ICTU and the employers' federation had decided that, where there was a predominance of people who wanted to see the Pope, workplaces could close and use that as a floating day. But in his letter Mattie said that there would be no 'collective sectarianism', no votes to coerce religious or other minorities who didn't want to take the day off and see the Pope. Therefore, officers should resist attempts to enforce collective religious holidays and defend the right of individuals of all religious persuasions and none to dissent from them.

There is a feeling in Ireland that sectarianism is something that begins when you go over the border to Newry. In fact, James Connolly said that partition should be opposed because it would lead to 'a carnival of reaction, north and south'. I rang Brother Merrigan and told him he was the twentieth-century personification of the United Irishmen and that Wolfe Tone would have been proud of him. 'Flattery won't get you anywhere,' he said. 'Just go and get it implemented.'

A small group of Protestants – about a dozen, who travelled from Armagh – worked in the Echo factory. When the question of using floating days for the papal visit came up I made the union's position clear to both members and employer: if people were sent home that day, I would claim a day's pay for them. The vast majority of people in Echo wanted to go to Killineer to see the Pope, but there was a small minority who didn't. They were sent home because the production process couldn't operate with so many people absent. I claimed pay for them, but the company said it wasn't their fault that everyone else went off to see the Pope. I took the case to the rights commissioner.

While we were waiting for the case to come up, the management of the company changed hands and someone was sent over from the United States to represent them at the hearing – someone with scant understanding of Irish culture, to put it mildly. The commissioner was Con Murphy, who could be quite conservative in his religious outlook. Before the case actually opened, the American acting for the company said that he had no argument with the union, that it was 'the goddamn Pope' who created the problem. Con Murphy just slammed his hand down on the table and, before a file had even been opened, asked me what I wanted. I told him I wanted payment for the people who went into work that day, and he gave it to me.

It was a small piece of enlightened trade unionism, looking after a minority, expressing the idea of progressive republicanism. The words were never mentioned, but those were the values underpinning our argument, and credit for that must go to Mattie Merrigan.

In the Dundalk office I found the 1916 minute book of the local NUDL branch, which existed up until the 1920s when it merged into the TGWU. The minutes for April 1916, kept by the officer who used to visit the branch from Derry by train, said something like: 'Many members are missing from the meeting. Everybody knows where they are. The matter was not discussed further.' I can guess where they were, because there was a plaque on the door of the union office commemorating the fact that the few people who went from Dundalk to take part in the Easter rising left from that point.

The H-Blocks was a huge issue in Dundalk. One of the prisoners, Paddy Agnew, was elected as a TD in Louth in 1981. It was taken up by the Trades Council on a motion from our branch, and I strongly supported the hunger strikers. We had half-day strikes every week in Dundalk during the hunger strike, the whole town every Thursday with big meetings. And geography matters: you could do things in Dundalk you couldn't in Dublin. There weren't as many stoppages in Dublin, although the remaining car workers stopped. The Provos didn't have sufficient roots in the trade union movement then to make it a class issue.

We had huge difficulties with the union in Belfast. Bobby Sands was a vehicle builder and in the NUVB, so he was our member. But the vehicle builders' branch in Belfast was mixed, and we were never able to get support for the prisoners there. We supported them through ICTU motions on a civil rights basis, but it probably would have split the union if we were to take a political, republican position. I saw letters John Freeman wrote to the Sands family, and the funeral benefit he paid out to them. I would have had a stronger view on the national issue than Freeman, but I wouldn't have been able to do as much if I was servicing members in Portadown. But where we could support the hunger strikers, as in Dundalk, we did. There wasn't the same level of support in Dublin, because it wasn't as much of an issue for the working classes.

In 1982 I spoke at a big H-Block meeting in Dundalk alongside Bernadette Devlin. Hundreds of women knelt down and said the rosary at the end. A pal, Liam Mulready, said, 'Ah, there you are now with the rosary brigade, and you never opened your mouth!' But I felt total empathy with these women coming together to express their sympathy as young men were dying.

I was in an organization called Trade Unionists for Irish Unity and Independence (what an awful name!) and attended the 1984 ICTU in the Ulster Hall as a delegate. A Loyalist organization picketed us, handing out a leaflet accusing us of being sectarian Catholic bigots for bringing the demand for a united Ireland into the trade union movement. Yet a united Ireland has absolutely nothing to do with sectarianism. I still want to see an Ireland where Britain has no role. I don't believe the British government has any rights in Ireland. Connolly's description of partition leading to a carnival of reaction is true, but it doesn't tell you how to get out of it once it's been established for decades, eating into the fabric of society and people's consciousness.

Brendan Hodgers was a shop steward in Echo who later became an official. When his wife Sheila was diagnosed with cancer, the family were told that she wouldn't be able to conceive during treatment. But she did get pregnant and the hospital refused to give her the X-rays needed to see how the cancer was developing. Her mother asked if I could do anything for her. I don't know if Sheila Hodgers would have wanted to have an abortion, but I do think she should have had the option.

Sheila Hodgers died on St Patrick's Day 1983, right in the middle of the abortion referendum. I remember listening to the debates on television while trying to help with the practicalities of this appalling case. Channel 4 News interviewed her husband – a good shop steward and also on our executive – who said: 'If you were in a hospital run and owned by the Jehovah's Witnesses, you would expect them to give you the option of a blood transfusion rather than imposing their own belief on you. Being in a Catholic hospital shouldn't impose things on you.' One of the most dreadful things ever done in Ireland was the eighth amendment to the constitution. It was shameful for Haughey and Garret FitzGerald to entertain the groups who were pushing for that amendment. We set up a fund for Brendan Hodgers to take a legal case and he was subsequently awarded a settlement.

Two years later, in 1985, Mary was admitted to St James's Hospital for the birth of our third child, and subsequently moved to the Coombe Hospital. I was up visiting her on the Sunday. Suzanne was staying with her grandmother, and Louise, who had just started secondary school, was returning to Dundalk with me that night. Around midnight there was a knock on the door: a garda announced that we'd had a baby – a little girl – and everything was fine. Delighted, I went back to bed. About an hour and a half later, the garda returned – there were problems and I should go straight to the hospital. I got Louise out of bed and we drove back to the Coombe. There had been difficulties with the birth, oxygen starvation and other complications. Emma, as we called her, only lived for four days.

This had a terrible impact on Mary and I. On the fifth or sixth day after Emma's birth, Mary suffered a heart attack in the hospital. They say tragedies come in threes, and on the Sunday I was with Suzanne and Louise at their grandmother's house when Louise collapsed with a burst appendix, requiring an urgent visit to Dr Steevens' Hospital. That week had started wonderfully with the news of Emma's birth, but change comes quickly. You can go from light to darkness in a second. Emma was buried in the Angels' Plot in Glasnevin, with only Mary's sister and myself in attendance.

Mary's illness was protracted and serious and it took us a long time to get things back to normal, but in a strange way it brought us closer. We did follow up the case and I discussed it with solicitors, but I don't know what we would have got out of it. We weren't interested in money. The hospital could have handled it a lot better than they did, but that was the way things were at the time. It was simply down to human error.

TWELVE

The Labour Party are a nice, respectable, docile, harmless body of men – as harmless a body as ever graced any parliament.

Seán Lemass

As an official in Dundalk I dealt with all types of people, including beef barons Larry Goodman and Hugh Tunney. They were formidable adversaries. I set up a combine across all the Goodman factories with the ITGWU and the Workers' Union of Ireland, which Goodman refused to recognize. We were looking for a wage increase of 15–20 per cent.

Goodman said: 'There'll be no overall settlement. Every settlement has to be agreed with each manager.'

'Nobody here is going to settle for a penny less than anyone else gets. Hell will freeze over first. I won't let other officials get more than I get for my members, and the same goes for them too. We're all going to get the same,' I countered.

Goodman replied: 'The managers can all agree individually to give you the same. If each comes to the same deal, fine – but every man will be responsible for it.'

'I don't care what theological fiction you want to file it under for your own purposes, but as far as I'm concerned it will be a collective agreement,' I replied. We faced him down and got our deal.

Both sides would go off for something to eat during breaks in the talks in Liberty Hall. Goodman was the kind of man who would never bring his people into a hotel for food; he'd take them to a burger joint and he'd make a virtue of the fact. One night around 9 pm we were coming back across Butt Bridge during these negotiations while couples who were living together were holding a meeting in Liberty Hall as part of the campaign around the 1986 divorce referendum. I said to him, 'You're not giving us any money, but would you ever give them a few bob?' And right there and then on the bridge, he took out his chequebook.

'How much?'

I think I asked for £1000, which I passed on to the campaign. Goodman added:

'This is different. This is me personally, not my companies.'

The fella who flew Goodman's helicopter approached me and asked to join the union. He could have joined the ITGWU, but insisted: 'I'm joining your one. I want you as the official.'

I asked why he was only joining now after working for Goodman for years. And he replied: 'Because he's thinking of getting a night light for the helicopter so it can fly around the clock. I'm working sixteen hours a day as it is, and if he gets the night light I'll be working twenty-four. I'll need a union!'

Goodman once told me he lived on the average wage. Other officials scoffed at this, but I said: 'If you're telling me that you personally live on £90 a week, I believe you. But isn't it lovely to be able to make that choice? None of the people who work for you have that choice. That's why I want more than £90 for them.'

Frank Aiken's son, an engineer, told me he had toured the world with Goodman – including the Soviet Union and socialist countries – to look at methods and technologies of beef production. Goodman was interested in breaking into world markets. I once told him, 'You and I will never agree, Larry, we'll always be fighting and never be friends, but if the Red Army ever gets to Ravensdale I'll make you Commissar for Beef, because I do believe you understand the industry even if you don't always look after the people who make the money for you.' He half smiled – that was as near as we got to some sort of understanding. Things were very testy between us.

This was around the time it was alleged that he had a much closer relationship with Fianna Fáil than other meat companies and got export insurance from Albert Reynolds. In his defence, I think his idea of breaking into new markets was a good one. The state should have been more involved, but the idea itself was important. Other beef barons like Tunney were all over the place with a diverse range of businesses, and never gave the meat industry the single-minded attention that Goodman did. He was ahead of the posse in that respect.

One of our best shop stewards, Peter McAleer, a republican, worked in Tunney's. 'Your union is being represented here by a dangerous terrorist,' he called to tell me when he was made shop steward.

'Well, if that's the case, I have a phone number you can ring: 999. It's up to our members to choose who represents them,' I replied.

And he said, 'Congratulations, you've passed the first test. You're on speakerphone, and I have the man himself sitting opposite me.' That's the kind of character Tunney was. I was lucky I didn't react to his statement the way a lot of officials would have done.

I went to the Creighton Hotel in Clones to meet twelve workers from Grove Turkeys, a poultry producer in Smithborough. Smithborough is a blink-and-you'll-miss-it village on the Monaghan–Clones road, a bleak spot with little employment. Six of these lads joined the union, and you couldn't have better people, tough and wise to the ways of the world, but I was nervous for them. I remember telling them at the meeting, 'Be careful who you tell you're in the union. If the whole twelve of you only recruit one trustworthy person a week, that's great progress. Don't try and recruit everybody in one day. Don't be too open about what you're doing until you have the lie of the land.'

The following morning I got a phone call from one of them, Jimmy McLoughlin. 'We were going into work this morning, and we were all sacked. What will we do?'

'We put up a picket,' I replied.

Everybody walked by it. We only had six people on strike and the factory working perfectly without us so I applied for an all-out picket, which congress agreed to. The inspection of meat and poultry plants is done by organized labour, so if the inspectors respected the picket the plant would be in trouble. Some of these inspectors went to the union and said they were going to leave it for the duration of the dispute, and they went in and carried out inspections.

I met the workers in a meeting hall across the road. They wouldn't let my twelve members in, so I was alone with a few hundred workers all carrying their work knives. I told them: 'I will not accept that you won't work with somebody because they're a trade unionist. They have a constitutional right to be in a union. You will not get these people sacked for being members.' A roar went up. Their hatred of me was palpable and hostile, and they booed me down every chance they got.

Unbeknown to me they had taped the meeting and took a hand-written transcript up to Mattie Merrigan to complain about me, with my speech repeatedly interspersed with 'Grove Turkeys workers: Boo! Boo! Boo!' Mattie somehow knew Frank Cosgrove who owned Grove Turkeys, and suggested that I talk to John Mitchell, the leader of the shop workers' union IDATU. I knew Mitchell to be a good left-wing official, unpopular with the executive of Congress but OK by my standards.

I went to see him. 'Can you do anything for me, John? I'm fucked.'

'What do you want me to do?' he asked.

'Can you black the turkeys and chickens in the supermarkets, tell the supermarket workers not to handle them?'

He took out a dictation machine. 'Will this do?' He switched it on and dictated, 'Memo to all shop stewards: black all Grove Turkeys products in all supermarkets.'

He switched it off. 'Do you want anything else?'

That was a Thursday, and I was in the supermarket in Dundalk with Mary on the Friday. A woman in front of us had a Grove Turkey product in her trolley. The woman on the till said, 'Ah no, they're blacked. You'll have to get something else.' The woman just went and put it back on the shelf and got some other turkey. That's when I realized that we could win this thing.

Cosgrove agreed to talk to me and to send the case to a rights commissioner. One of the people advising Cosgrove's crowd was a former union official. I saw him around the negotiations although he wasn't directly involved. One night I met him in the car park as I was going home. 'You're going nowhere with this. You should have more sense,' he said.

'Are you in the business of breaking unions now?' I said.

'Ah, no,' he replied, smirking, 'but this is a lost cause. You're just left with a few fellas and they're all Provos.'

'Do you think they're Provos?'

'I do, yeah.'

'And you still feel completely OK with what you're doing?'

The penny dropped. He went as white as a milk bottle and I never saw him again. There is a special place in hell for somebody who helps break a strike.

We wanted our members reinstated with payment for the time they were out. It was clear they had been sacked for being in a union, a fact Cosgrove never denied. He was an innocent abroad in that sense, although he was also a nasty piece of work. The recommendation was that they be taken back to work and with back pay. Cosgrove accepted this but said he didn't want them back just yet. I said that I didn't care as long as they were getting paid. They ended up getting paid for a good while, including over-time, even though they weren't working.

But then one of them called to say they wanted to go back to work, and so the twelve of them did – as they were entitled to do – and everyone else walked. There we all were, in the middle of the yard, all these other workers with their knives wandering around. Some Provos came up in a car and took photographs for *An Phoblacht* – propaganda was already being spread that the strike was organized by the Provos.

Cosgrove came up from Dublin. I knew I had the strike won because the place had ground to a halt. He accused me of starting trouble but I was firm. 'These people want to work. You're paying them, they're entitled to work, and they want to discharge their duties. It's you who has a problem, because it appears all your loyal workers have gone on strike. My men are here to work, and that's the way it'll be.' He had pumped all his people up against us and now he couldn't let the air out of the balloon. 'I'll leave you to think about that, but my lads are going in now to start work,' I concluded.

Just as I was going out the door, Jimmy McLoughlin pulled me aside. 'Mick, I know you think we can win this, and maybe we can, but I don't want to work with them.' I let out a string of insults, calling him all the names under the sun. 'You wouldn't work with them!' he added.

'I would, because I'd organize them. We have them now, and you'll be the organizers. He has a factory full of chickens waiting to lay eggs and the place is stopped. He's fucked, he's going to crack, and a day will win this thing.'

'I don't care, I don't want to work here.' They were all of the one mind. Cosgrove had even proposed segregating them, but I could appreciate how the atmosphere would be difficult.

I got them a good settlement, generous redundancy and favourable references. We made sure that they were the first people to be employed when vacancies came up in Tunney's. And I told Cosgrove I wanted recog-nition for the union in Grove Turkeys, that if the place was ever organized the ATGWU would be the union. I addressed the works committee: 'I think you made terrible mistakes, but you're not my enemies. These are the redundancy terms I got for my members, and none of you can rely on getting anything like that if you're sacked. If you're ever in trouble, I can look after you.' And Cosgrove deducted a pound a week from each of them to pay the union members' redundancy! They all joined the union before long. It was a very unusual dispute.

Things were different in rural areas, but it's still the class struggle. Workers are workers: they may be ignorant sometimes, but they are the human material with which we must build a new world. One thing I found dealing with workers in rural Ireland is that a lot of them had small farms and could take time off for other tasks: a strike might last longer because it was sunny and people wanted to cut the hay. Even in Fiat there were fellas who ran small businesses from a garage in a back lane, which could keep them going during a strike – but I always wanted money off them to support the strike, because not all workers were in that position.

Most of us who left the Communist Party in 1976 joined the Labour Party. I didn't – but not for any ideological reason. I had no antipathy towards it but I simply didn't like the culture. It wasn't a commitment, like the union or the Communist Party. Labour felt like a very middle-class organization. I didn't join until I had to and I always say that I never joined the Labour Party: I joined the executive and I joined Labour Left, which is different.

There was a big *rí-rá* going on in 1982 at the time of the see-saw elections, with Haughey in and FitzGerald out, then FitzGerald in and Haughey out. The argument was always whether Labour should fight elections on a joint platform with Fine Gael, or separately and do a deal afterwards. O'Leary, the party leader, wanted a joint programme with Fine Gael. Jimmy Tinkler, who represented the ATGWU on the administrative council of the Labour Party, voted with O'Leary. I raised this in our branch and wrote a letter to head office objecting to the union's representative voting that way. Mattie wrote to Tinkler asking for an explanation, but he replied that he wouldn't explain himself because he wasn't elected by the votes of the ATGWU alone. I said to Mattie that we shouldn't put him forward if he wasn't even going to explain his actions to us after voting against the union's policy.

Brother Merrigan, in his imitable style, put it to me straight. 'All right, you want to pull Tinkler down, but what are you going to put in his place? You'd better join the Labour Party, and we'll put you forward for the Administrative Council. Your arguments would sound better if you were in the party. Go down and get yourself a membership card. I can't join, they expelled me twice.'

I joined up. I got myself nominated for the Administrative Council and went down to a conference in Cork where I met a fella I hadn't seen since school, Noel Byrne from Kylemore Road, and got his votes. Then I met Billy Wheatley, who I had worked with in the car factory, and got a few votes off him, and votes from different unions. I amassed the lowest vote, but with transfers from all over the place I got elected. Could this be a serious organization if you got elected after only two weeks, I wondered? But I was happy and enjoyed my time there. I spent ten years on the AC, much of it in government with FitzGerald. Being in a coalition with Fine Gael was difficult. There were huge rows, over the 1985 Anglo-Irish Agreement for example, and Labour had an appalling attitude to the national question. There was also a row over Phil Flynn, when Barry Desmond said he'd have to get his office fumigated if he ever talked to a Sinn Féin member as a union representative. I went for him over that.

Labour Left produced a magazine, controlled about 40 to 50 per cent of the votes at the annual conference, and had a good few TDs who were in and out with us. Some of the stronger ones were people like Emmet Stagg and Mervyn Taylor. Some were reformists who just wanted a bit more edge to the reform, and others were just furious because they didn't get a job, or were afraid they'd lose their seats. Michael D. Higgins was a great supporter of Labour Left. At that time the Labour leadership dealt with him by basically saying he was mad, as happened with Tony Benn in Britain. When you hear someone described as mad, you can take it that they're perfectly rational but making inroads. If I was making a criticism of Michael D., he could have been a bit more disciplined in his relations with us, because he was very individualistic. But on principled issues, where you had to take a stand, he was always there with us even if it sometimes took him a while.

We started a campaign for the leader to be elected by the party and I wrote a pamphlet arguing for that. A member of the Italian Communist Party, who was living in Ireland, designed the cover: I wanted a visual image of democracy, and she did a terrific picture with a load of hands going up. As I was going in to the party conference where the issue was to be decided, Úna Claffey from RTÉ told me: 'If your motion is passed, I understand that Dick Spring and Barry Desmond will resign as leader and deputy leader.'

'You're just giving me more and more reasons to get the motion passed!' I said. But that was never broadcast. When we won, Dick Spring took it personally. His argument was that the TDs had been elected by the people, were tried and tested, and knew more than everyone else knew. In the debate I said that was the politics of Marie Antoinette. All the parties made that argument then, although they've all accepted election by the members since, which shows you how the world has changed. I never foresaw that it would eventually lead to the likes of Pat Rabbitte becoming leader, but I do think it's better than having a leader selected by the parliamentary party. Our theory was that it would make the leadership more combative if they had to be elected by the membership, that it would be a useful tool for the rank and file to chasten them. We were trying to change the culture of the party, not just the rules, to get them to look at politics differently. It was the first time the unions had held together solidly against the party leadership, which was something of a watershed.

A lot of people in the party were being dismissed by Labour Left as right wing, but I insisted on ringing these people, meeting them and arguing with them, and I found that they listened and I changed some of their minds. Saying that people are beyond the pale and not worth talking to becomes a self-fulfilling prophecy.

All of us who left the Communist Party were in Labour Left. It was like being an entryist. I regarded myself as a communist and still do, even though I'm not in the party. That's my politics, my ballast, how I analyse things. I stood up and said something at a Labour Left meeting once, and Sam Nolan said something similar, and George Jeffares said pretty much the same, and Brendan Halligan said 'Oh, the CP are factionalizing.' In one sense he was right. We never met or discussed things together, but we were analysing things from the same outlook, which made it look as though we were meeting even though we weren't. Conspiring doesn't work. Shortcuts and sectarianism have played havoc with the potential development of the Left in Ireland, and it's still a problem.

I told Halligan: 'We wouldn't need to meet to be saying similar things. I analyse everything on the basis of Ireland's Path to Freedom, the first Communist Party programme from 1933. I believe that's the application, broadly speaking, of James Connolly's analysis to Irish history. That's what I try and do anywhere, in the union, in the Communist Party, in the Labour Party. What's the beef?' He was astonished, had never heard anything like it.

Halligan was an interesting character. He was in Labour Left but nobody trusted him because he had been with the leadership. The Right hated him because he was like Lucifer: he had been in heaven and left it. He threw in his lot with us and we didn't trust him either, but he was an amazing man to get an insight into politics because he had been in the inner circle. He became convinced that that coalition was a disaster and he wanted to fight it. He was an MEP, gave us lots of money to help with magazines and so on and was useful because he knew where the bodies were buried.

Michael Bell, the TD in Louth, wasn't with Labour Left but backed us on the election of the leader by the members. I remember persuading Eithne FitzGerald (who later became a TD) to support us, but when she heard that Spring and Desmond were threatening to resign, she came to me with her dilemma. I quoted Shakespeare's boatman: 'You do assist the storm' – in other words, shut up. There's a time for hesitation, and that's before you sign. Once you're in the trenches, you have to be like Marshal Zhukov: no stepping back, only forward.

I got on with the Dundalk Labour Party militants like a house on fire even though we didn't agree on anything. They were decent people trying to do the right thing but going about it the wrong way, a cross between a political organization and a religious sect. At meetings of the Labour Party

AC there would be a file of correspondence from councillors and so on: people could inspect it and raise anything they wanted to. No one did go through it, apart from Joe Higgins, who would read it all diligently with his little notebook in hand.

Joe was very much opposed to Militant's expulsion from Labour, although it has turned out well for them. I don't think the Labour Party would ever have allowed him to be elected. Together with people in Militant I used to organize May Day socials in Dundalk, with singing and poetry, something the Labour Party branches just don't do. They reduce everything to the local road crossing. We brought in a bit of outside thinking, but a lot of them would have no cultural dimension or vision to their politics, which is a tragedy. That tradition is there in Labour, but they've forgotten it.

I was opposed to setting up the Socialist Labour Party in 1977 in which Mattie was involved. He once said, 'How dare you tell me I shouldn't operate outside the Labour Party when you've operated outside it all your life?' It was a well-deserved smack in the mouth. I saw the SLP as a kind of Tower of Babel and didn't think they could make it work. I wasn't a great admirer of Noël Browne: he had huge individual motivation but would never fit into an organization that would tell him – or even suggest – what to do. I knew some of the left-wing groups who joined but didn't think they had the wherewithal to build a serious movement.

The huge opposition to the coalition helped Labour to survive. In 1987 we won 6.5 per cent of the vote and twelve seats, the maximum number you could get with that vote. That was enough to survive, to build on.

There was a big left-wing group in the Labour Party arguing for a different point of view. We were trying to impose the structure of Eurocommunism on the Irish Labour Party, but I don't see rural Labour TDs ever being Eurocommunists! When the Labour Party collapsed after the coalition, it had a sense of itself because of the political impact we had made inside the party. Nowadays the Labour Party is a shell of its former self. It does have some roots in the country and a connection with the trade union movement, but a question mark hangs over its future.

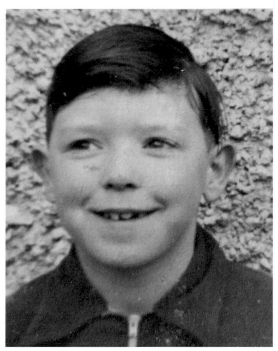

Mick O'Reilly aged six, at home in Ballyfermot, Dublin, 1955 (photo: Anna Ashmore, eldest sister).

Mick and his sister Anna on O'Connell Bridge, Dublin, 1958 (photo: Arthur Fields, *Man on the Bridge*).

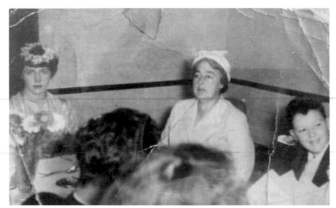

Mother, Lucy (*née* Watts), with Anna *(left)* and Mick, aged twelve,
at his sister Teresa O'Reilly's wedding in Birmingham, 1958.

Mary (*née* Brien) and Mick O'Reilly on their
wedding day, Inchicore, Dublin, 1972.

Meeting of the Connolly Youth Movement (CYM)
at the Irish Workers' Party HQ, Dublin, c. 1968.

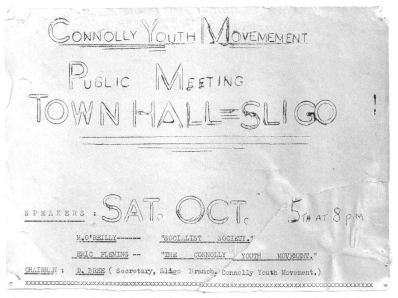

Flyer advertising the forming of a branch of the CYM in Sligo, 1968. Chairman
Declan Bree later became a Labour TD and independent socialist councillor.

Protest against entry to the Common Market, 1972.

O'Reilly speaking at a recruitment rally for the
Communist Party on Abbey Street in Dublin, 1973.

O'Reilly at a conference on Marxism with *(from left)*
Sam Nolan, Joe Deasy, Bernard Browne and Eamon Dillon,
at the ATGWU office on Abbey Street in Dublin, 1984.

Protest against the downgrading of services at
Louth County Hospital, Dundalk, 1989.

Jazz as Gaeilge

The distinctive voice of Melanie O'Reilly

SOUND: 12

Ca

The film cine

VIS

The two union officials involved in the Packard talks, Mr Brendan Byrne (left) of SIPTU and Mr Mick O'Reilly of the ATGWU, at the Labour Relations Commission in Dublin yesterday. Photograph: Peter Thursfield

Packard talks break off as workers quit assembly line

'A day left' to save plant

By Padraig Yeates,
Industry and Employment
Correspondent

TALKS between Packard management and unions broke off dramatically at the Labour Relations Commission last night after a number of workers at the company's plant walked off the assembly line, despite an appeal by their union representatives to maintain the 41-hour working week.

Government sources indicated last night that there was still "a day left" to try to save the plant, but it would have to be on the basis of the peace formula, agreed yesterday, which had enabled the talks to take place.

Mr Kieran Mulvey of the LRC is understood to have adjourned

found for renewed negotiations.

It seemed at 8.55 p.m. that talks which the LRC and the Government had been seeking all day would at last take place. But within a matter of minutes, the personnel manager at the plant, Mr Jim Dohn, received a call on his mobile telephone and left the LRC talks with the rest of the Packard management team.

Before leaving, he told union representatives that they should contact their own people at the plant, according to shop steward, Mr Dick Payne.

LRC, reviewing the situation.

It is understood that one of the reasons for the unfavourable reaction by members of the workforce to the appeal of their unions was a communiqué issued to all employees by the plant's managing director, Mr David Schramm, yesterday. It began by warning the workforce that any breach of the productivity agreement would lead to the non-viability of the plant. He also referred on several occasions to the "fatal" effect of a return to the 39-hour work week from the

which only a short time earlier seemed to contain high hopes that Packard could be saved. At 6 p.m. the unions had agreed, with obvious reluctance, to lift industrial sanctions against the company in order that direct talks could take place. Last night's meeting would have been the first such talks in a week.

Immediately after the agreement on LRC talks, Mr Michael O'Reilly of the AGTWU and a number of shop stewards left the offices of the Department of Enterprise and Employment in

first of a series of information meetings and let the employees know they should continue normal working to allow talks to take place.

However, at the first of these meetings, there was very strong resistance to suspending industrial action.

Meanwhile, another group of union representatives had gone to the Labour Relations Commission to be available for talks there. The secretary of the shop stewards committee, Mr Liam Berney, said that they had decided to accept the company's demand that the 41-hour week be retained because of assurances from the Minister for Enterprise and Employment, Mr Bruton, that all issues raised by the

AMALGAMATED

NEWS

JUNE 2002

DEFEND DEMOCRACY IN THE T&G

Jimmy Kelly, General Executive Council member.

"When the General Executive Council is debarred from discussing the suspensions and dismissals of the two most senior Irish Officers, how can we look our members in the face and tell them democracy is alive and well in the T&G?

I urge all union members to discuss and take up the issues raised in this newsletter and to defend the democratic and militant tradition of our union."

Jimmy Kelly

Pic. Michael Gallagher

John Curran from Belfast addresses Dublin trade union activists last year.

Shop stewards meeting

Over 50 ATGWU shop-stewards from Dublin turned up to a meeting in May organised by the 3/90 Branch oñ the ATGWU with speakers Mick O'Reilly, Eugene McGlone and Jimmy Kelly (GEC representative).

Nobody could have imagined the first hand accounts of Bill Morris's abuse of power in relation to both Officers and the Irish Region.

The meeting demanded the immediate reinstatement of Mick and Eugene and resolved 'to set up a campaign to restore democracy throughout the Transport and General Workers Union and decide the future of the Irish Region, the ATGWU.'

A steering committee was elected to co-ordinate the campaign. The first task is to ensure that Mick and Eugene's case reaches the membership of the TGWU and that the democratic structures of the ATGWU are not undermined any further.

What the Amalgamated Support Group stands for:

Contact the Amalgamated Support Group through Des Bonass (Dublin) at 087 792 5120 or John Curran (Belfast) at 02890 222 836

◻ The immediate restoration to office of Bros. Michael O'Reilly and Eugene McGlone.

◻ The withdrawal of the imposed disciplinary procedure used to dismiss Brothers Michael O'Reilly and Eugene McGlone.

◻ The continued tradition of the ATGWU as a trade union independent of the employers.

◻ The Irish Regional Committee to convene an ATGWU Conference to discuss and resolve the above issues.

◻ Full support for the proposed strike action of the National Officers Committee.

Financial Appeal

The recent decision by Bill Morris, General Secretary, T&G to sack our Irish Regional Secretary, Michael O'Reilly and Irish Regional Organiser is both undemocratic and unjust. Both Officials are appealing against their flawed dismissal, and we are requesting you for financial support so that a proper professional defence can be made on their behalf, and for their reinstatement. We have been denied access to the facilities of the ATGWU and have no income other than your support.

The importance of the success of this appeal will effect the whole of the Irish Trade Union movement and beyond. All details of this dispute can be seen on the www.shaftingtheatgwu.org website.

Big or small, individual or on behalf of Union branches or organisations please show your support.

All donations will be gratefully accepted and acknowledged and should be sent to:

The Mick O'Reilly and Eugene McGlone Support Fund TSB Abbey Street Dublin 1 Sorting Code: 990601 Account Number:71619739

For further information please contact Des Bonass 087-7925120.

Amalgamated News: The Amalgamated Support Group campaigns for the restoration of Mick O'Reilly and Eugene McGlone to office following their dismissal, 2002.

AMALGAMATED

NEWS

MAY 2003

DEFEND DEMOCRACY IN THE T&G

Vote
TONY WOODLEY
for T&G
General Secretary

Tony Woodley

"Members want a union that will do the business - not a business union"

Tony Woodley

· · · · · · · · · · · · · ·

See our website at

www.tonywoodley.com

or phone

Des Bonass,

Dublin

@ 087 792 5120

or John Curran,

Belfast

@ 02890 222 836

June 26th 2001 marked a disgraceful day in the history of T&G in Britain and Ireland. Our General Secretary, Bill Morris embarked upon an onslaught of our proud traditions by placing our Irish Regional Secretary, Mick O'Reilly and our Irish Regional Organiser, Eugene McGlone on 'precautionary suspension' whilst only informing them of his charges an entire month later.

By Tony Woodley, Deputy General Secretary

Due to the mighty resistance of the T&G membership to the imposition of these disciplinary procedures by Bill Morris and the integrity of both Mick and Eugene a good victory of re-employment for both Officers was achieved in March this year.

The T&G has played a vital role in Ireland since 1922, representing workers North and South, giving voice to the unity of our members

interests as opposed to employers, Governments and the blind alley of sectarianism.

Mick and Eugene upheld this tradition at all times and were leading a vibrant, growing and confident T&G in difficult circumstances in Ireland.

The last two years has seen a reverse of this growth in membership, confidence and strength. The T&G must remain a Union that is prepared to fight back against the employer and represent our members' independent interests at every level.

As General Secretary I will recognise the established rules, that the members in Ireland have the responsibility for governing the affairs of the Union in Ireland, who I trust and have always upheld T&G policy throughout the Irish Region.

I am committed to the reversal of any injustices, which occurred during the imposed disciplinary procedures, which will mean using all my power and influence as General Secretary to restore Mick and Eugene as Regional Secretary and Regional Organiser.

As General Secretary I will consult with Branches, District Committees and the Irish Regional Committee about the number of offices and where they should be - or remain to be, in any case I am committed to take our union back into towns and cities that we have evacuated.

I will work with the Officers' National Committee to develop a new and fair procedure that can be agreed by all, ensuring that we never again go down the path of division.

I will lead a united, proud and powerful T&G.

Dismissals overturned
Mick and Eugene thank supporters

Pic. Michael Gallagher

Mick O'Reilly and Eugene McGlone

We would like to take this opportunity to wholeheartedly thank the Officers' National Committee, shop stewards, members, friends and colleagues in the T&G in Ireland and Britain, the hundreds of trade unionists in other unions who have contacted us offering support and solidarity, and the general public who have supported us since our "precautionary suspensions" 22 months ago.

It has been a very trying and testing time not just for us as individuals, but more so for our families. The aforementioned support and goodwill helped us get through, what can only

be described as one long nightmare, and for that we will always be grateful.

We are anxious to draw a line under the past and move on. With a new General Secretary of the T&G to be elected this May, it is essential that we all put the traumatic events of the last 22 months behind us and look forward to the future and the task of rebuilding our Union. This election is the most important in the history of the T&G.

We unequivocally support Tony Woodley in his campaign for election as T&G General Secretary. Tony Woodley is opposed to part-

nership with employers and government, he believes in partnership with the membership and he rejects business trade unionism. As Tony states in his election manifesto for General Secretary:

"We are going to re-claim our culture, once again becoming a union fighting for the members, a campaigning union, a growing but above all a united and tolerant union where fear plays no part. I promise you if elected - I will make that difference."

We are both happy to be playing a part in our great Union once again!

Amalgamated News: Mick O'Reilly and Eugene McGlone thank supporters following the announcement of their reinstatement, 2003.

O'Reilly with Eugene McGlone, Deputy Regional
Secretary of the ATGWU, Belfast, 2005.

O'Reilly with the late Joe Deasy, the last living
councillor who served with Jim Larkin, 2007.

O'Reilly seated with *(left to right)* Jack McKay, David Ervine, William 'Plum' Smith, Billy Hutchinson; standing up *(left to right)*, Maurice Cunningham, Norman Cairns, Davie McMurray, Eugene McGlone, Alison Gribben, Billy McCracken and John Curran in discussion with the Progressive Unionist Party in the Transport House, Belfast, 2008.

O'Reilly with lifelong friend Bernard Browne at a
social function in the Dublin ATGWU office, 2011.

O'Reilly commemorating the 1913 Lockout with *(from left)* Jack O'Connor, Eoghan Runane, Jimmy Kelly, Ger O'Laoghaire and others outside Leinster House, Dublin, 2013.

Mick O'Reilly, Declan Bree and Liam Mulready at a
CYM celebration in Wynn's Hotel, Dublin, 2014.

Mick O'Reilly today, 2019.

Recruiting poster by Conor McHale, addressed to archaeologists, 2014.

Mocked-up cover for *From Lucifer to Lazarus* by Conor McHale, 2019.

THIRTEEN

Yes, Dev, that's quite true; if I had been in your place there'd have been a great many people who would have left the country. But they would not have been the same people!

Peadar O'Donnell

Oh, we
Who wanted to prepare the ground for friendliness
Could not ourselves be friendly.

Bertolt Brecht

The national wage agreements resulted in workers coming in and saying: 'Fine. That's what the government gave us, but what are you going to get for us?' No one understood that these agreements were actually negotiated by the unions, meaning workers had no sense of ownership. If you go into a factory and spend two or three days arguing the toss, threatening the employer, have four or five meetings with the workers where you air the issues, they will eventually accept the outcome, heave a sigh of relief and go back to work. But if it comes down on a conveyor belt from Dublin, announced by some politician, they've no sense of involvement in proceedings. Neglect your negotiating skills and you lose them. Muscles atrophy from lack of use. When you do this for a whole generation of trade unionists, you end up with a movement with a head and no body. And that's what happened to the trade union movement: we've lost a lot of the culture and lore of how things are done.

We had about seven or eight years of free collective bargaining, but it was in the worst possible circumstances. It wasn't the ICTU who pulled out of national wage agreements in 1979 but the employers because of the world recession. In a boom, employers want partnership to hold down wages. In a recession, they want to hold down wages on their own. Whatever happens, they want to hold down wages: that's what employers do.

The average settlement we got in Dundalk was around 22 per cent, but that didn't translate into higher living standards. This led to some people in the trade union movement arguing along the lines of, 'See, that's what you get with free collective bargaining – a pay rise, but because of inflation and taxation it ends up bringing a decrease in living standards.' They got away with plugging that line because the establishment and the media were in agreement. The real comparison of different methods of wage negotiation is the application of them in the same set of conditions. We know what a national agreement would have produced, because negotiations fell down when the unions couldn't get 12 per cent.

Curing inflation by building a Left government is part of having a vibrant trade union movement. Free collective bargaining might be a reflection of capitalist politics and couldn't bring about socialist policies, but I haven't noticed socialist policies developing from national wage agreements. Free collective bargaining is a reflection of the differentiation of classes. The idea that that doesn't exist and we are all in it together is a denial of capitalist structures and of reality itself.

I've always believed in having a national wage agreement with the government as an employer. There are thousands of people who work for the state, and it's the biggest employer in the country. The private sector is another matter. It should always lead the negotiations, with the public sector following, because the private sector is competing and exporting. That's common ground understood by Left and Right in the trade union movement, although in practice the time devoted to public sector workers was sometimes excessive compared to the problems we had in the private sector. I don't believe in this 'private sector versus public sector' nonsense. There are a lot of low-paid people in the public sector, for example.

How do you deal with the weaker sections of the movement? Not by settling for a flat-rate pay increase, tail-ending conservative governments and lending trade union support to the totality of their economic and social programme. But that's what we did. If you want a Labour movement where people can think and act, you have to free them up to do so. It's dangerous to build a tendency for everything to be done by the official or by the General Secretary or by the ICTU, because when it collapses you're left with nothing. I feel thoroughly vindicated for opposing national wage agreements. I think they were disastrous for the trade union movement.

The question of job creation could not be tackled by wage restraint, nor would that necessarily attract capital for investment purposes. The primacy of job creation requires a political alternative, a Left government. Developing the indigenous economy where we can win big foreign markets requires a creative role for the state.

We need to develop worker participation. It would make a big contribution to the economy if we had more import substitution. I argued that we should expand the area of free collective bargaining to negotiate with the employers about alternative indigenous sources for the supply chain. We should look at this not just from the perspective of the individual enterprise but from a national and workers' perspective. Free collective bargaining could involve more than just looking after wages. It would expand the control of workers and politicize the trade union movement. People ran a mile whenever I raised this point. It requires a leadership that has the political ambition to do such things, and the Irish trade union movement don't see things like that. That that's why we've ended up in the heap the trade union movement is now, because we've forgotten simple, basic things like going out, talking to workers, finding out what the issues are.

The Programme for National Recovery in 1987, and all the partnership agreements that followed, didn't lead to the redistribution of wealth or a more equal society. We were simply sustaining governments in carrying out their own programmes when we should have been fighting to put a programme supported by the broad left before the people. After all, the Social Contract in 1970s Britain – which I would have opposed – was made between the Labour government and the unions, and the employers were just told they had to pony up the increase agreed.

If partnership gave unions a voice in the corridors of power, it was never heard above a whisper. It's just rhetoric to claim that our voice was getting heard in government. Getting government to advance towards the trade union programme involved letting them know that you'll be bringing a lot of your members next time. Partnership did the opposite: it was a big wet blanket over the trade union movement.

These agreements survived the participation of the PDs in government. There was no redistribution of wealth while they were in government, and the trade union movement was on board with that. It was all about cutting tax on a universal basis – a very right-wing idea – and we bought into that ideology, to the detriment of the movement. Partnership grew, but it never expanded into social policy, taxation, job creation – all the areas we said it would. What it grew into was manipulating the trade union movement into endorsing the programme of governments, which they in turn used quite cleverly.

We had very few strikes in Ireland, but notwithstanding that, the 1990 Industrial Relations Act (which was not that far behind some of the things Thatcher was doing at the time) was brought in with the collusion, agreement and support of the trade union movement. There's a wonderful pamphlet on this by Pat Rabbitte and Éamon Gilmore, *Bertie's Bill,* with a picture on the cover of Bertie Ahern with a monkey at the zoo – a savage attack on the politics and meaning of the Act. The Labour Party was in opposition then but were prevailed upon by Congress not to oppose it.

One of the fundamental things the Act did was to outlaw strikes called to support a single member. Anyone who ever organized anything anywhere understands that it's usually one person who starts something. Collectivism doesn't fall from the sky; it has to be built by individuals. Cold recruiting – standing outside a factory handing out leaflets – doesn't work. When someone comes into your office with a problem you tell them, 'Camouflage yourself. Don't get caught until we get a number of members together.' The foundation stone of the trade union movement is Larkin's great slogan: 'An injury to one is the concern of all.' He understood that sometimes you have to build around an individual.

The Act also banned political strikes. The strikes I was involved in to enhance the EEC protocol protecting car workers' jobs would have been illegal under the 1990 Act. You also have to have a ballot for any industrial action, even for a go-slow or an overtime ban. It stunted the capacity of our class to move smartly on issues, and killed spontaneity. And these ballots can be challenged in the courts by anyone affected, even people outside the dispute itself. Caution is required once everything is legalized. I've never met a judge who drove a bus or worked on a building site or had an understanding of the world of workers. They understand the law, but they don't understand its ramifications for workers.

We tried to make the case against partnership deals, but we were in a minority. The increases for public sector workers were much the same under partnership as otherwise. Sometimes a special agreement was made containing a top-up for building workers, for instance. Of course, there was a huge propaganda machine in favour of partnership: you might have 40 per cent of SIPTU members voting against a partnership deal, and 90 per cent of ATGWU members. Put together it's a majority, but it wasn't counted like that.

Congress wanted to move away from 'comrades' or 'brothers and sisters': 'colleagues' was the new word. Our members were to be regarded as consumers of the product of trade unionism. Partnership required new thinking towards employers, but while we may have renounced class struggle, they certainly didn't. They're very straightforward about it; they're in the business of making money. Every time there's a boom, we're told we have to restrain wages. Every time there's a collapse we go back to free collective bargaining. Would it never dawn on people in the unions that we should have free collective bargaining at a time when there's lots of money about? It's baffling that people do that again and again.

There's no case for workers not facing government and employers with one voice. The ATGWU had a big membership in Northern Ireland, and if we left the ICTU would almost not exist there. That would please a lot of reactionary people in the Unionist community who would have regarded our affiliation to the ICTU as joining an organization in a foreign country. I often think the leadership of Congress took us for granted.

The idea that we enhanced our position through social partnership is nonsense: they enhanced themselves at our expense. It certainly didn't leave Ireland better off socially or politically, it just propped up the status quo. The best you can say is that the trade union movement was sold a pup. Would people have got more money without social partnership? I suspect they couldn't have got any less the way the economy was growing. But that's not the point: the big weakness of partnership is the ebbing away of the self-reliance and skills on which the movement is built.

We moved back to Dublin from Dundalk in 1988 and I began to work with the ESB and engineering workers. The ESB was fascinating and, unlike other places, highly structured in its negotiations. Worker participation was excellent. They knew how to look after their wages and conditions, and had some very good negotiators among the shop stewards. The union visited the members at every power station at least once a year. I remember going to Turlough Hill up in Wicklow, the most peaceful and tranquil place. The file on Turlough Hill was the smallest I ever found in the union, with about three letters in it. Everyone was involved in the administration of the power station, an oasis of calm in a sea of misery.

I ran a campaign to keep open a depot in Ballyfermot. Although the ESB eventually closed it we did manage to have the workers, still based in Ballyfermot, driven to their new jobs around the country. Whether that's a sensible use of resources is debatable, but our job is looking after members. That wouldn't happen in a better-planned economy and a more egalitarian society (and one of the reasons I'm in favour of socialism is to stop such conflicts) but in a deformed society such as the one we live in, you're driven to do things like that.

Jimmy Tinkler, the ATGWU official in the ESB and secretary of the group of unions there, created all the union structures, had a fantastic knowledge of the industry and knew how to use the system after over thirty years as an ESB official. He was deeply religious and we had totally different outlooks, but we got on and he was a very effective official. We had the odd argy-bargy over how to do things, but nothing personal or malicious. I never found it difficult to take advice or learn from people, and I don't think you should close your mind to them because of disagreements on other issues.

The three unions that really mattered were the ESB Officers' Association, ourselves and the Technical Engineering and Electrical Union. It was a very effectively organized group of workers, probably the best I've come across apart from the car workers. They have their own internal disputes mechanism, an industrial council with an elected worker, a management representative and an independent chair. As well as that, a worker from the place where the dispute happens is elected to the panel discussing it, as well as a local manager. This derived from the Fogarty report after the strikes of the late 1960s, and I think it's better than the Labour Court system. They still manage to have strikes now and then, of course!

ESB workers have a lot of power but they don't misuse it. Trade unions have the power to *stop* something, but can that be used creatively? If OAPs are having their pensions cut, should the trade union movement not look at using its stronger sections to defend them? It's difficult to imagine that at a time when it seems they hardly use their power even to defend themselves, but I would argue that the job of the ICTU is to shape a culture in the movement that would see the potential for using its power in a more collectivist manner. To do that, you would have to engage in a major educational programme among the public and the members themselves.

Does a union not have a responsibility to do more than reflect its membership? Larkin didn't just reflect his members; he led them. Leadership requires thinking and formulating policy in a collectivist socialistic direction. If the movement doesn't find a role like that it just drifts along with the flotsam and jetsam of history.

The collapse of communism from 1989 on is the most profound thing that's happened globally in my lifetime. Eric Hobsbawm correctly states that the twentieth century started in 1914 and ended in 1991. It was about Russia, to quote Woody Allen. Everybody in the world was influenced by the Russian revolution. It was the most important event in twentieth-century history, unique and without parallel, an audacious event that turned the world upside down, just as the French revolution had. The collapse of the Soviet Union and all that has gone with it has had a profound effect, and anyone who says it didn't matter to them is either stupid or unconscious. The world needs a countervailing force to America.

Communism as it was practised in the Soviet Union and eastern Europe had huge weaknesses. It always intrigued me how the Soviet Union could be so competitive when it came to armaments and outer space, but when it came to televisions, fridges and all the things ordinary Russians relied on they seemed rather lackadaisical. This was an oversight. The West kept Russia on her toes in relation to infrastructure, but the country lapsed into complacency when it came to looking after her own people. There are many things about the Soviet Union I admire – culture, the way old people are cared for, the education system, health services, transport – but Soviet emphasis on the quantity and quantity of consumer goods was non-existent. Gorbachev tried to deal with that, but how do you get incentives to service people well? You have to have openness, criticism, ways to measure outcomes, and a lot of that was lacking in the socialist countries.

The Soviet Union should have reformed. The advance of socialism in western Europe would have created circumstances where there could have been more democracy within the Soviet Union. That would have still meant upheaval and change, but it would have been change within a broad socialist culture, with something of socialism being retained. Instead its development has set back the socialist project for generations. I would have preferred to see the Soviet Union evolve in the direction of Sweden, or some kind of social democracy, but instead it collapsed into awfulness. People went along with Gorbachev's reforms but in truth only paid lip service to them. So-called Communist Party officials transformed themselves over-night into business advisers and sold the place left, right and centre.

The politics I learned in the Communist Party are, largely speaking, the politics I have retained, with the exception of my criticism of eastern Europe. But I was always careful what I said, and would defend much of what went on there. Given my industrial background a lot of people were amazed at my sympathy for Eurocommunism, but had the Eurocommunists made a breakthrough – if Czechoslovakia had successfully reformed, if Italy had gone socialist – then the state apparatus that surrounded Stalinism would have collapsed in a better way, leaving some remnants of socialism.

People drew the astonishing conclusion that with the collapse of the Soviet Union we had the end of history. I think it shows the opposite – history never stops and there is always struggle and movement. Building socialism is very difficult now (and it was easier to imagine a socialist world then) but the crisis of capitalism is still there. The financialization of capitalism is in many ways retarding development of the productive forces, and those contradictions are still in place. There is a revival of Marxism intellectually and in the socialist movement, and a collapse of European social democracy. To look for a bit of Keynesianism is a revolutionary act, which will topple the establishment these days, just as it was a revolutionary act in Northern Ireland to look for 'one person, one vote'.

What is lacking in the Left, however, is unity and cohesion. Competition is healthy, and you don't have to be enemies. I despair of the Far Left's tendency to fall out with each other.

I didn't see Mary Robinson's presidential campaign in 1990 as all that earth-shattering. She won more because of the hames that the Fianna Fáil candidate Brian Lenihan made of the election than some change in public opinion. Robinson wasn't a radical; she left the Labour Party because it wasn't pro-Unionist enough. She did represent modernity and a more enlightened society, but it wasn't a huge transformation. Michael D. Higgins, on the other hand, represented positive left-of-centre social democratic values.

Labour went into coalition with Fianna Fáil in 1993 and I now regret my support at the time. Fianna Fáil had a grip on the working class because it did things the working class saw as important: reform, taxation and its ideology on the national question. Labour should have left on all those questions, instead of which the leadership saw themselves as representing Dublin 4, making sure that Haughey or Reynolds or Bertie Ahern didn't support republican demands in Northern Ireland. They should have been more republican, which could have worried Fianna Fáil and appealed to their base.

Labour Left ceased to exist and Labour left that coalition over a row. It's one thing to go down in history for leaving something, but not to go out of power for something no one can remember. It eventually left them out of government for fourteen years, during a prosperous period when things could have been done. From their own perspective as a parliamentary party, it was a disastrous mistake.

FOURTEEN

Any contemporary of ours who wants peace and comfort above all has chosen a bad time to be born.

Leon Trotsky

When Mattie Merrigan retired as Republic of Ireland Secretary in 1986, I canvassed for the job. I was waiting for it to be advertised, and after he went to his last meeting of the regional committee, I asked him if they had set a date for interviews. 'They filled it. Freeman gave it to Charlie,' he said. In other words, the Irish regional secretary John Freeman had appointed Charlie Douglas.

I hit the roof. I wrote to Freeman and the regional committee and every branch in Ireland. Without wanting to speak ill of Charlie, who everyone liked, people shouldn't be getting jobs just because they're decent people who have been around a long time. I'd said to Charlie: 'If you get the job this way, you will be beholden to Freeman. You should actually insist on an interview for your own good.' He looked at me as though I had two heads.

John Freeman was furious but eventually sent me a letter of apology. Ray Collins in the London office of the TGWU told me to frame it because it was the most unusual letter anybody in the union had ever received. Most people thought that row would destroy me in the union. It put me at loggerheads with Freeman, who would have an influence on who would eventually replace Charlie and who would get his own job when the time came. Apparently, I had burned all my boats with Freeman, humiliated him into writing this letter, and my career in the union was finished. I didn't see it like that. As it happened, a vacancy came up in Dublin in 1988 and Freeman had no problem appointing me. Everyone thought I had overplayed my hand, but it had quite the opposite effect. After a few months of huffing and puffing, Freeman became my best pal.

I knew John Freeman first in the Communist Party. I think he was in the party more because of the influence of the British Communist Party in the union, rather than seeing things as an Irish communist. He told me once that when he went to school on the Shankill Road, the only Irish song he ever heard was 'Abdul Abulbul Amir', but I would regard him as a republican. Like any regional secretary, his speeches were written for him, but he was always much better when the speech went into his back pocket and his working-class instincts came to the fore.

He used to work in Shorts aircraft factory, and once in the early days of the Troubles when the Loyalist leader Billy Hull was trying to set up a separate Northern Ireland trade union organization, he attacked Hull at a meeting. He was taken out of Shorts in the back of a car with a blanket over his head. I think he stayed with Jack Jones in London for a couple of months, and then with Séamus Geraghty in Dublin. It was a difficult time for him. He was right in saying what he did, but it wasn't the most sensible decision to do so.

He always claimed that Andy Barr didn't support him enough, but in my experience, Andy Barr had a backbone made of steel. I was in Belfast at a regional committee meeting at the time of the Ulster Workers' Council strike in 1974 and got one of the last trains back to Dublin. There was a terrible atmosphere. It was as near to fascism as I ever got. The strike was based on intimidation at first, but once it got going the Protestant community swung behind it wholeheartedly. The first days were decisive, and the Labour government didn't act strongly. Len Murray of the British TUC came over to march with a group of trade unionists against the strike: some of them would have been murdered if he hadn't been there. I admired those who led that march, and Andy Barr was one of them.

When Charlie Douglas retired as the Republic of Ireland Secretary in 1991, I became his successor. I had a bit of a profile from my involvement in Labour Left. We'd launched a May Day Manifesto for the 1990s signed by socialists, republicans, communists, trade unionists, environmentalists, Labour and Workers' Party members, and I lobbied the union for their support. I got on famously with John Freeman. When he was president of the ICTU he asked me to run for the Congress executive, and I was elected. Some people thought that, as Congress president, he wouldn't want his own union opposing a partnership deal he had negotiated, but when I told him I was going to oppose it he encouraged me to go ahead. I was involved in strikes, even strikes over the H-Blocks, and he never interfered.

I once spoke at a huge meeting in Manchester in support of a British withdrawal from Ireland alongside Bernadette Devlin and Ken Livingstone. I talked about the spancel on the trade union movement caused by not being able to talk about the issue and said that British unions should look to the Irish movement as a whole, not just their own members in the North. When the meeting finished, a Sticky came up to me (official republicans were nicknamed 'Stickies' because their Easter lilies didn't have pins in them). 'I heard what you said and I have it taped, and I'm going to report you,' he said.

'Do you want the address? Do you think I came over here in secret?' I replied. Freeman got the tape but never tried to stop me speaking. Later, when I ran for regional secretary, an old leaflet from Trade Unionists for Irish Unity and Independence was resurrected and circulated around Shorts to undermine me.

Whenever people rang to ask whether they could do this or that, I told them to go ahead and do it instead of asking permission. If they had a tough nut to crack and wanted to discuss it, fair enough. But they're paid to think, and if they're getting someone else to think for them what are they doing?

Freeman ran the union from Belfast. As Trotsky once said, anyone desiring a quiet life has done badly to be born in the twentieth century, and that's even more true of Belfast in John Freeman's time there. He held the union together during that period, which was a hugely complicated task. It's easy if you represent one side of the conflict, but not if you represent two. It would have been a disaster if Northern Ireland had descended into war in the workplaces, with Catholics being driven out on a mass scale like they were in the 1920s. John Freeman was involved in that achievement. I would have been critical of him – for example, I supported the MacBride Principles against employment discrimination and he didn't – but I never regarded him as a sell-out, whatever that might be.

The Republic of Ireland Secretary was a very powerful position in the ATGWU. Some positions in the trade union movement are powerful because of the rules surrounding the job, but some are powerful by the sheer personality of the person who holds them, or even the indifference of others to them. The power of the Republic of Ireland Secretary really came from the energy of Mattie Merrigan. He was more than just a district official; he was a regional secretary and a leader. Brendan Halligan once rang the TGWU General Secretary Jack Jones to complain about Mattie threatening to disaffiliate from the Labour Party, and Jones just said to him, 'I never interfere in arguments between Irishmen. Resolve it yourselves, and don't ring this office again.'

Working with our members in Team Aer Lingus was a dream, they were so incredibly well organized. Aircraft maintenance involves a lot of mobile work and the company wanted to separate them from Aer Lingus and set them up as a semi-state company to compete in the world market. When Team was set up they extracted irrevocable, absolute guarantees that, if anything happened to this company, they would go back to their jobs in Aer Lingus. A lawyer looking at this deal said that he had never seen such a watertight agreement. I liken these agreements to the treaties made with the American Indians, where Sitting Bull was promised that he would have his land as long as the sun shone and the wind blew.

The shop stewards took the view that they would try and make the new company work. They weren't just oppositionists: they wanted worker participation, which caused a lot of conflict. Gramsci used to say that if you wanted to move away from wage slavery, just dealing with pay and conditions, you had to look at what, how and why you manufacture. There was a germ of that social dimension in the Team battle. The company didn't have a strategy for engaging the talents of the workers, and resented the level of information and participation we were looking for. There were difficulties over pay and hours, largely because of the seasonality of the business: working through the summer months and taking your holidays in January is best from a business point of view, but it's obviously a problem if you want to take your kids on holiday.

There were three officials called O'Reilly – Frank O'Reilly from the TEEU, Tommy O'Reilly from the National Union of Sheet Metal Workers, and myself. A host of other unions were also involved, including Michael Keating from the Automotive General Engineering and Mechanical Operatives' Union, and SIPTU had a few members, but the primary official was Frank O'Reilly, who had a terrific rapport with the shop stewards.

Mark Fielding, who now represents ISME, worked for us as a consultant in the Team Aer Lingus dispute. He did a great job. At one meeting he put together a list of bullet points for shop stewards who were going in to argue our case with management. One of them, Paddy Finnegan, said to him: 'I build planes. When I put them together, they're checked by an inspector, and I have to make sure that they'll hold together when they hit turbulence. You've given me this document, and I'm bringing it into a place where there'll be a lot of turbulence. Will it hold together?' Fielding said it would, and Paddy said: 'Good enough. Let's go.' It was a terrific exchange, a craftsman looking at how an argument is constructed. The company brought in John Behan, who had a reputation as a union buster. The word on the street was that he was connected with the Fianna Fáil government – his son later became a Fianna Fáil TD. During a dispute over pay we had a lockout, or at least the workers were all laid off. In order to maximize disruption, we walked around the airport roundabout and stopped there for five minutes out of every fifteen. You can imagine the impact that had on traffic into the airport and on flights. Union rule books also gave us the right to call meetings of maintenance workers. These were methods we used short of having a full-frontal strike, but none of them were rooted in a ballot. We just did them, which leaves your arse hanging out the window as far as legal protection is concerned. Many of the unions were nervous about this. If someone can prove that you delayed a plane being repaired or taking off, the solicitor's letter will be looking for damages with lots of zeros at the end.

We eventually reached a settlement. The following day a big industrial relations conference took place in Dublin. Michael Keating, who hadn't actually been involved in the negotiations, taunted Behan that he had been asleep and let the unions wipe the floor with him. In the end the company reneged on the agreement. We spent three or four months trying to work out a solution but eventually lost the dispute, probably due to divisions on our own side.

North County Dublin was strong Fianna Fáil territory at that time, the airport was a big part of the vote, and ministers would look for meetings with Aer Lingus. The local TD, Ray Burke, spoke at a street meeting in Swords, urging the workers to go back to work. Congress didn't like the fact that government were meeting us directly without going through them. I told the workers to just go down to Bertie Ahern's clinic and that infuriated the ICTU leadership even more. Because the strike was lost, the workers weren't able to go back. The guarantees were worthless because Aer Lingus no longer carried out maintenance and there was nothing for them to go back to. A small number did return and although they were getting the craft rate, they were doing different work altogether. People who had joined Team after it was set up had no right to join Aer Lingus, so there were divisions over that.

It was a defeat for an important kind of trade unionism. An advanced system of worker participation was later developed in Aer Rianta, but the workforce there were too passive to take advantage of it, whereas it would have fitted the Team Aer Lingus workforce like a glove. It's one of the 'what ifs' of industrial relations history to speculate on what advances would have been made had those two elements coincided. Months later I parked my car in Connolly Station before getting the train to Belfast and found it clamped on my return. The young fella who came out to take off the clamp turned out to be the son of Danny Murphy, a Team shop steward – he was reluctant to charge me but at the same time couldn't get into trouble with his boss.

The dispute in Packard in Tallaght was completely different. I had a most peculiar relationship with Packard. General Motors closed down Reg Armstrong's in the 1970s and we occupied it. The workers eventually settled for enhanced redundancy and the right to apply for jobs in Packard. Those jobs, putting circuits together and harnesses for cars, were well paid, but lousy compared to what car workers were used to.

When I came back to Dublin from Dundalk, Packard had imposed a no-strike clause after a dispute. Instead, workers had to go through an internal grievance procedure with elected workers' representatives. This backfired when Mattie Merrigan was elected, taking away the company's absolute power – and if there's one thing General Motors understand, it's power. It was the beginning of the latest phase of globalization after the collapse of the Soviet Union, and GM wanted to close Packard and move to another country. I was looking at a horror story.

At union meetings a group of the women would always sit up at the front of the canteen, knitting. I was always reminded of Sydney Carton on the guillotine in *A Tale of Two Cities*, thinking, 'It is a far, far better thing that I do …' You would be negotiating all week and reporting back to a meeting on the Saturday, and the first question would always come from one of these women: 'You gave us a report that lasted ten minutes, and you were a whole week with the company. What are you holding back from us?' They were terrific, tough as nails, and I enjoyed working with them.

The world was changing. We wanted to go towards a different form of production where there would be more individual responsibility and less monotonous assembly line work. We tried to get the company interested but they had already made a decision to close. Pat Rabbitte, Mary Harney and Mervyn Taylor were TDs in Tallaght as well as ministers of one sort or another at the time, allowing us to punch above our weight. We probably kept the place open three or four years longer than the company wanted to through sheer doggedness.

One of the concessions we had to make when Packard threatened closure – one which nearly broke my heart – was to work an extra hour and a half a week without pay. The workforce agreed to loan those hours to Packard on condition that this debt would be paid, and in the event of the company closing those hours would count as time and a half in redundancy considerations. It shows that if you're organized you can still fight back, even when the other side is one of the biggest companies in the world.

GM used to sponsor the Irish football team and I tried to hire a helicopter to fly a message over one of the matches with a banner saying 'Pay the Packard workers' but we couldn't get any takers. We then tried picketing garages, but were threatened with legal action.

Official Ireland didn't like Packard management because they didn't abide by Labour Court agreements and saw themselves as a higher authority than the moguls of social partnership in Ireland. They were ruthless employers, in the business of making money, and if the Labour Court stood in their way, they would just go through it. Packard were allegedly involved in the coup that put Pinochet in power in Chile in 1973, so why would the Irish Labour Court frighten them? During a demonstration when Packard were refusing a Labour Court recommendation, a senior civil servant said to me, 'Dear oh dear, Michael, you should grow up. Whichever way this goes, it's the job of this state to keep the empire sweet, and General Motors is the empire.' That was very revealing of the mindset at the highest level.

That same civil servant also worked with John Bruton when he was Taoiseach. One year, Bruton addressed the ICTU conference. I was a delegate, and Mattie Merrigan attended as an ex-president. We were in the hotel bar late one night when Bruton came in with a fawning entourage, a pint of Guinness in one hand and a whiskey in the other. When he spotted Mattie, he broke away from his hangers-on and made a beeline for us. 'Mr Merrigan, I'm delighted to see you,' he said. 'I never agreed with a word you said, but I always had great respect for you, one of the few decent socialists I ever met. How are you?'

'What the fuck is Muttonhead doing at our table?' bellowed Mattie, who was a bit deaf.

In the end, GM paid the agreed terms. The final meeting was bitter because everyone at Packard lost their jobs, but they knew that everything that could be done, had been done. We were given a huge standing ovation in the canteen. That's as well as any case can end.

When Bill Morris was originally standing for General Secretary of the TGWU in 1992 I went up hill and down dale in support of him. In fact, I had a row in Belfast with people who felt it was wrong for the Left to run a black candidate because he wouldn't get elected. I thought Bill's time had come and we had to take on reactionary attitudes. They were afraid that the right-wing press would mangle us with a black candidate.

I didn't support Morris for a second term; I supported Jack Dromey, who was more right wing. He was closer to Tony Blair, while Morris was a Gordon Brown man. I preferred Dromey: he spent most of his life on the Left, had great knowledge of Ireland, worked hard, and was slightly to the right of Morris, but maintained power through his self-confidence and not through repression. Bill lacked self-confidence and had a tendency to be autocratic in office. Much of the Left had the same attitude, but they didn't understand the nuances. Where does authoritarianism come in when you're examining the Left–Right divide in a union? It's crucial to have a General Secretary with a capacity for tolerance. I should have done more to get Dromey elected, not just because of what Morris did to me, but because he was a disaster for the TGWU. People were afraid to stick their neck out, and that kills a union.

FIFTEEN

The Transport and General Workers' Union was founded in 1922 by amalgamating fourteen unions set up into eleven powerful regions across Britain and Ireland, each responsible for their own administration. Ireland was always one region, and the Irish executive would decide on matters relating to Ireland. They also had trade groups representing workers in one industry over a large area, with their own secretary. Sam Kyle, a left-winger from a Protestant background, was the first Irish regional secretary from 1922–49. Norman Kennedy, also a Protestant, had just left the Communist Party when he got the job in 1949. It was a profound change for the union to have an Irish secretary from the South, a Catholic and an open republican who had always campaigned for British disengagement from Ireland.

Three people went for the job when John Freeman retired in 1997: myself, Eugene McGlone and Liam McBrinn, all Catholics. Liam McBrinn's father had been interned as a republican and been on the ITGWU executive. Liam would have been a Communist Party type, and some people joined the party in Belfast in Freeman's time to get a job in the union. They wouldn't have been through the battles that other communists had fought in the

131

union. The one political label doesn't necessarily do justice to everyone, and that generation were very weak.

The campaign was enormous. There were thirty-six or thirty-seven members of the executive and I had a list of them in alphabetical order, saying where they went to school, what their politics were, who could influence them, and so on. I was determined not to be John Freeman's enemy or his candidate either. I went to the various groups for support: Trotskyists, British Labour Party members, old friends in the British Communist Party – you name it, I went to them.

The Irish Communist Party showed little interest in the process. Their attitude was that three left-wingers were going for the job and they would go along with whoever the union chose, but I was sceptical. Myself and Mick O'Riordan shared the same local and I decided to raise it with him there. 'What's this?' I asked. 'You've no interest in who gets elected?'

'Oh, the party took a decision,' he replied.

'I know, but what's really going on? This is me you're talking to.'

He laughed. 'Well, they think McBrinn is going to get it.'

'He will if you have that attitude. I want you to do something for me: make a phone call to Kevin Halpin, the British CP's industrial organizer, and tell him you're supporting me.'

'But we took a decision. I'm sixty years in the party, and I've never gone against a party decision.'

'I know, Mick, but there's a first time for everything. Will you do it?'

And he did. I think I can claim to be the only person on earth to get Mick O'Riordan to deviate from a decision of the party's political committee. He told me not to tell anyone, but I think I can now.

Eugene McGlone pulled out of the race. He had a Hard Left vote, but it was small. What the right wing had in mind was to vote for Eugene; then I would be out and my soft left vote would go to McBrinn. The only way that could be defeated was if Eugene jumped ship, which he did. He made his move in the interests of the wider Left. I wasn't aware of all this, only that my vote was beginning to fray at the edges.

I rang Eugene after he dropped out. 'Thanks very much,' I said. 'Send me down what you have, and I'll see what I can plagiarize for my speech to the executive.' He was quite shocked but I was determined to win the thing.

I was to go to London on Tuesday. The interview with the executive was on the Wednesday, and I got a phone call from John Freeman about 10 pm the previous Sunday. He told me how important it was to prepare. I told him I mightn't make it.

'You will make it!' he roared. 'When you go into that room you're speaking for Ireland, and for the whole Left in the union. Speak your truth and fear not! Be like Daniel and go into the den! I'm going to bed now. Good night.'

I had to laugh. He was impressive – all his Irishness was coming out.

When I went to make my speech to the executive I could see panic on the faces of the bureaucracy. They're not often beaten, and every regional secretary Morris wanted, he got. The regional secretaries ran the union with Morris and he regarded them as managers, with the members as customers. I had twenty minutes to speak. I stood and made a rip-roaring speech. I had every word written down and timed to perfection, but as always, I threw out the notes as soon as I started.

Then I was questioned by the General Secretary, the organizer, Margaret Prosser, and the Deputy General Secretary, Jack Adams, who was supporting me – thanks to Freeman's influence, I think. It was all going well until they asked me a question about rights for disabled people, cast in terms of British law. The day before there had been a row in Ireland over the Equal Status Bill brought in by Mervyn Taylor to provide greater accessibility for disabled people, which had been found unconstitutional by the Supreme Court because it impeded property rights. I answered the question in relation to that legislation because I wasn't able to address the situation in British law.

The minute I left the room Morris jumped on this, claiming that I didn't know the position on disability rights. But Ivan Monckton from Wales countered: 'He did know. He answered the question in relation to

Ireland, not England. He's applying for a job in Ireland.' That lost Morris huge ground.

Monckton, who worked for the agricultural section of the TGWU, was spending his summer holidays in Kerry. In an attempt to win his vote for McBrinn, he was invited up to visit the Moy Park chicken factory in Portadown. A woman called from Morris's office in London: 'We've got Ivan over there, and he needs to get to Portadown. What's the best way, Mick?' So I got the number for Ivan's campsite and told him that I'd give him a lift up if he got as far as Dublin. As we were driving up, an item came on the radio about Joe Higgins supporting the right of kids in Ballyfermot to keep horses. Of course, for someone over from Britain to hear a socialist member of parliament campaigning for horses for everybody was a great story. We got on famously.

When I dropped Ivan at the office in Portadown I told him: 'They're going to try and nobble you for your vote. They'll put huge pressure on you but just kick it to touch, because I'm looking for your vote.' I know someone who worked in the factory and told him that when he saw Ivan Monckton, he should tell him how good I was, which he did. Ivan couldn't believe the support I had in Portadown, so I got his vote. Sometimes it's the minutiae that decides a course of events.

I supported the Liverpool dockers and made friends with them; they had a good case and were treated badly. We organized huge collections for them in Ireland. They came over to Drogheda to stop a boat being loaded there for Liverpool. They slept on the floor of the ATGWU office in Drogheda and then came up to Dublin the next morning. I told them that if you sit down on the road for no more than fifteen minutes and then walk for another fifteen minutes, you're not breaking the law. Don't ask me where I got that idea from. We went from the Four Courts down to the docks, sitting down on the road every once in a while. It caused chaos, and we managed to disrupt the loading of the boat.

This was just after I became regional secretary, and in fact the day after my appointment I went over to a huge demonstration in Liverpool. There were twenty thousand people there, but no other regional secretary or national official of the TGWU. Someone asked me to do an interview on a webcam – I didn't quite know what a webcam was, but I did it. We had to start as we meant to go on, and if we were going to annoy Morris we might as well do it early. I was nervous for my future in the union, but I wasn't going to stop supporting them just because I was regional secretary now.

A group of our members in Belfast clubbed together, took the ferry to Stranraer, slept in a van and drove to Liverpool for the demonstration. A republican pipe band was playing Irish rebel songs and some of the Belfast lads asked me to stop them. I told them to ask the band themselves. In Belfast I might have had a word, but I couldn't go over to Liverpool and tell people what to play. McBrinn was due over with the Belfast group, but once he lost the secretary's job, he took his money back and pulled out of the trip.

Dockers from all over the world supported the Liverpool men. Three of them flew to New York docks to intercept a strike-breaking ship. They put a picket on the docks – turning a big ship around is surprisingly easy – and all the New York dockers supported them. The ship was sent to Louisiana, so they hopped on a Greyhound bus to stop it again. They were arrested and thrown into jail. People like that are the salt of the earth, what unions are all about. We collected thousands for them. I'm proud I stood with them, and they presented me with a commemorative picture by way of recognition.

They lost, but set up a worker-managed co-op in the dock, which some of the car factories used. There were inevitable legal difficulties with the dispute, but Morris could have looked for international solidarity, for workers in other countries with fewer legal restraints to act in support.

When I became regional secretary in 1996 John Freeman was delighted. I don't know whether he was delighted for me or delighted that Bill Morris had been defeated, because himself and Morris didn't get on. He asked me whereabouts in Belfast I was going to live, then added: 'Your name is Michael O'Reilly. You come with a certain baggage. Go on up to west

Belfast and live with your own.' I ended up living just off the Falls, not far from where he lived himself.

I told me once: 'The one thing Unionists up here detest is if you try and be smart with them, because they'll know exactly where you're coming from.' My attitude towards Unionist workers was always that I would go fifteen rounds for them if they were in trouble with their boss, and I might even throw an extra punch just to prove I was on their side, but I wasn't going to change my political views.

Before I went to Belfast, I was a republican socialist, but once in Belfast I became a socialist republican. Sectarianism was always present. I went to a debate at the West Belfast Festival and on my home I met Peter Black, a member of our executive who was in the Irish Republican Socialist Party. He introduced me to someone from the Irish National Teachers' Organisation, an immaculately dressed man whose name I can't remember. I shook his hand, went home and thought nothing of it. The next morning at work a member from east Belfast came up to me. 'You were out last night and you were talking to the chairman of the IRSP.' That's Belfast for you!

I used to listen to the Northern Ireland news on the drive up from Dublin. One day I heard that an abortion advice centre in a Protestant area of Belfast had been burnt out – of course, opposition to abortion is one issue that unites a lot of people in the North. I arrived at work and called the women's officer to say that we needed to get a statement out about this attack. 'You know, in some ways the Protestants are worse than the Catholics,' I said.

'What do you mean?' she asked.

'The Protestants read the Bible literally. The Catholics have run states and held power and they read between the lines. But these Protestant sects have never had power, and they're hopeless.'

It was only an observation, but she was shocked beyond belief and went round telling people how awful I was. I heard that comment quoted back to me again and again. I became afraid to say what I thought. As I was leaving for Dublin after a meeting with members in Shorts, I said, 'I'll be on my way now – I have to be down in the capital this afternoon.' Driving through Newry I got a call from the office telling me that was an awful risky thing for me to be saying. I remember telling my secretary Valerie Cornish, a Methodist:

> I could inadvertently behave in a sectarian manner without even knowing it. I am now appointing you, by battlefield promotion, as my adviser on all matters ecumenical with full authority to tell me anything you think is right or wrong. I'm not going to stop being myself – I am from the capital of Ireland, and I don't believe in anything religious – but I am aware that I'm walking on eggshells here.

I did get some funny looks, especially with my accent.

I went to Stormont for a meeting with the DUP minister Willie McCrea about transport. It was a freezing cold day, and all he gave me was a glass of orange. He went into a rant about supermarkets, big business, lack of government empathy with small farmers and small business people. We used to have a term in the communist movement, 'objective anti-imperialists'; Willie McCrea was an objective anti-imperialist apart because of his problem with Catholics. Down South he would have been in Fianna Fáil – people in that party have the same outlook as him.

The day Harland & Wolff closed, the workers went to march. One of the officers called to say that the officials would be meeting the march at the Ulster Hall. But I was going to march from the shipyard. I was making the point that I didn't like that style of trade unionism, the lads marching and us officials meeting them afterwards to tell them great things. During the march I was told that I couldn't be on the platform in the Ulster Hall. I was going to argue my point, but decided that would be the last thing workers wanted on the day they were losing their jobs. It was subtle, bureaucratic sectarianism.

I also met the best people in Belfast, people who would always confront sectarianism. During the 1998 referendum on the Good Friday Agreement I covered the wall of Transport House in Belfast with a huge slogan saying 'Vote Yes'. A few members said they'd leave the union, but I told the officers and the regional committee that we can't talk about anti-sectarianism and then sit on the fence when an agreement like this comes along. We had to take our courage in our hands and participate. In the end, 90 per cent were behind it and people on both sides said fair play to me for putting my money where my mouth was. There was a cute hoor minority, but that exists in the South too – in fact, you find less of it in Belfast.

The TGWU had an executive meeting in Belfast to celebrate the peace process, and I arranged with the lord mayor to organize a civic reception. It was all very formal with people dressed in Beau Brummell suits and all. At one point the call was made: 'Be upstanding for the toast to the Queen.' I hadn't thought this through at all and just drank the toast, knocked back a large Black Bush.

That night I introduced Mattie Merrigan to Bill Morris. He and Morris had a bit of an argument, then Morris moved on to talk to other people in the room. I went to ask Mattie what he thought of him. 'He's a fucking coconut!' he said. Mattie was slightly deaf and talked very loudly. A coconut is an American phrase for an Uncle Tom, used by black people to describe black people who don't stand up.

Because a regional secretary is more involved with administrative and political affairs than actually negotiating with employers and so on, I kept on some work like that, bits and pieces to keep me sharp, but it took up an inordinate amount of my time. I come from the Larkin school of administration and I admit that expense accounts would not be my preferred Sunday afternoon reading. I had good people working on that side of things and I told them to bring something to my attention if it jumped out at them, but otherwise things worked well on autopilot.

Liam McBrinn would oppose me for the hell of it. The unprecedented level of coverage I received raised the profile of the ATGWU from a small, obscure organization to a major media force. But if I got publicity for disagreeing with other unions Liam would accuse me of splitting the movement, whereas if I was agreeing with other unions, he would accuse me of having no original ideas. Whatever way the cat jumped, he'd have a saucer of milk for it. A couple of officials didn't like me, but there were no deep factions within the ATGWU in Ireland.

I opposed Freeman because he didn't support a strike or a campaign, not because I wanted his job. Much of modern politics is about management rather than policies, personalities rather than ideas. This also goes on in the trade unions. I'm not saying I never had a personal row with anyone in the movement, but I always tried to keep to the issues.

I always expected Bill Morris to settle down and work with me once I got the job as regional secretary. He sent me and other officials and administrators to a management school in Loxborough House near Birmingham, where someone explained about 'customers' and so on. Absolute rubbish. At the end of the week one person had to sum up what we thought of it all, and of course I got the job. I gave it to him from the shoulder, but Morris took it personally. I might only see Bill once a year. I was working away in the silo in Belfast. A regional secretary's job involves four or five meetings a day, committees, boards, disputes and issues, and worry about what Bill Morris thought of me hardly crossed my mind.

Whenever I rang the office in London, I'd always say, 'Tell him it's the Foreign Secretary.' I wasn't just being funny – I was conveying a message. I can't remember one thing we wanted to do in Ireland that the TGWU in England didn't sanction. At the end of the day, if you're sitting in Smith Square in London you don't spend your days wondering what people are doing in Cadbury's in Coolock, or on the Shankill Road. Northern Ireland is even more baffling to the English than the South of Ireland.

I had a long talk with Morris about Sinn Féin in the car from Belfast to Enniskillen where he was opening a union office. We discussed my attitude towards partition. I assured him that it had no effect on my ability to represent all our members, but he was nervous. The next time I met him, he told me: 'I've just joined the Friends of Sinn Féin in London. I met this fella Martin McGuinness, and he's a fantastic man.'

We had a big row at the union's conference in 1999. There was a motion down from the 3/90 branch calling for equality for the Irish language, extension of civil rights, a second chamber in the North based on civil society, which was actually set up, along with lots of different community groups. These policies would have advanced the union much further than the ICTU's position.

While the armed struggle was going on we had motions in the union calling for British disengagement, which would be dealt with by an executive statement. This would be put before the motions, and if it was passed all the motions fell. It was a tried and tested bureaucratic method of crushing democratic debate. Sometimes I went along with it, because there was no way of actually pushing that kind of motion through the union. One year I was presented with an executive statement by Bill Morris to which I objected. He said that this was the way the issue had always been dealt with, but I told him: 'In case you haven't noticed, things have changed. The peace process is being discussed in the Dáil, in the US Congress, the European Parliament. Is the Transport Union the one place it can't be discussed?' In the end he agreed not to do anything until I came back from the ICTU conference, which was going on at the same time.

But on my return he had gone ahead and issued an executive statement to the delegates. Our delegation were ready to walk out if their resolution wasn't going to come before conference. I told them I would move the statement, then use the rest of my speech to tear the guts out of it and get it defeated. Instead of walking out, we could win.

And that's what happened. The last sentence of my speech was: 'I support the executive statement.' But it was defeated by five to one, and Morris went mad. The most left-wing group of the union bureaucracy are the industrial secretaries, while the regional secretaries tend to be more right wing. When I finished the speech, all the industrial secretaries jumped up and applauded. I was given a spontaneous standing ovation, with about three-quarters of the hall on their feet. The regional secretaries just sat there, Morris apoplectic with anger. Then, to put a cap and cloak on it, I went into a pub to have a cup of tea, and Morris came in after me. And the whole pub, a couple of hundred Scousers, all started singing 'When Irish Eyes are Smiling'.

That day I had an article in the *Morning Star* and he sent for me to discipline me over what I'd written. I replied that John Freeman wrote an article in the *Morning Star* every year at conference time, and no one stopped him. 'He had permission,' he said. This was news to me. Morris claimed it was a private session of conference, but my article dealt with the situation in Ireland, not the details of the conference. That cheap shot annoyed me no end.

People had warned me about Morris right from the start, but what can you do? Being on tenterhooks all the time will undermine you. I absorbed what people were saying, but then forgot about it because there was damn all I could do but get on with my life.

SIXTEEN

*Well, it won't be popular with the ICTU to say this, but Mick
O'Reilly of the ATGWU was the man who got it right most often
during the year 2000.*

Peter Cluskey

*That's like the cardinals voting against the Pope. I'm telling you
now, Morris is fucked. You'll be back.*

Mick O'Riordan

I took the view that the regional secretary acted for the whole of Ireland,
and remained involved in the southern side of things, thereby raising the
profile of the union throughout the Republic. I didn't add terribly to the
traditional arguments of the TGWU, but found PR people to place arti-
cles in the *News of the World* and *The Star*, even a positive editorial in *The
Sun*. The trade union movement is obsessed with getting into *The Irish
Times*, but frankly, you won't find many *Times* readers on a building site.

I interviewed a PR person called Marty Whelan who had a background in the Communist Party and had just finished working for Bertie Ahern and told him that if he could get a photograph and a statement into the *Evening Herald* within a week, the job was his. They duly appeared. It's very important to get into the papers that people read. The biggest correspondence I got from members was in response to an article in the *News of the World*, not any of the pieces I did for *The Irish Times*. I was also regularly in the broadcast media. Once you get a reputation for having something to say and you're reasonably representative, you're in.

During the early years of the Celtic Tiger we produced a pamphlet describing inflation as 'the acid that corrodes workers' wages'. David Hanly gave me twenty minutes on *Morning Ireland* to discuss it. When you're so isolated on the ICTU executive that you can't even get a seconder for a motion, you have to think of creative ways to initiate discussion, so I decided to use the media to create a debate and unashamedly lobbed in my bombs.

My opposition to the Nice treaty in the 2001 referendum annoyed other union leaders, but the fact that there was a minority taking a different view (which turned out to be the majority view in the country) did no harm. The trade union movement doesn't always have to have one voice, and the odd solo run is not the end of the world. If the movement gets into a totally establishment-oriented position, it has no future.

Healthy competition among unions is good for the workers. A multiplicity of unions in a workplace or sector doesn't matter if they all accept majority decisions – then you have unity in diversity, instead of uniformity at the expense of democracy. This was at the heart of the 2000 dispute over the Irish Locomotive Drivers' Association.

When ILDA members joined the ATGWU we were unfairly accused of poaching them. The train drivers joined us as individuals, not as the ILDA. When Iarnród Éireann took them to court, SIPTU wrote to the court to say they weren't members of theirs. Half of them had been in the National Bus and Rail Union, which is outside Congress, and therefore weren't covered by ICTU rules. I advised them join the NBRU, but they thought the NBRU was as bad as SIPTU. I only became involved in the dispute when it was almost over, once it became clear that they didn't have a union, and when Minister for Transport Mary O'Rourke urged one of the other unions to take them in.

Joe O'Toole, Des Geraghty, Peter Cassells, Peter McLoone and Dan Murphy confronted me at an ICTU executive meeting. I gave as good as I got. Dan Murphy, the thinking man's right-winger (who represented higher civil servants) was probably one of the most successful negotiators in the movement, but that was because the people on the other side of the table were his own members. I told him: 'I take particular umbrage at you criticizing me because you never worked, you were never sacked, you never stood in an industrial tribunal, you never carried a placard on a picket or went on strike. You know fuck all about this movement, and most of the people agreeing with you there are the same.' You wouldn't believe the amount of people who told me they wished they could have said that to him! I liked Dan Murphy, but he never had to fight his way up like I did. I had something to bring to the table, but all he could see was someone upsetting the applecart.

At one point I thought Des Geraghty had called me a Trotskyite. I stood up and said, 'Did you call me a Trotskyite?'

'No, I called you a troglodyte!' he replied.

'Oh, well, that's all right, then.' This brought down the house.

Standing in a daze on the steps of the Belfast office that day, 26 June 2001, I looked behind me to see Eugene McGlone coming out and immediately felt a bit better.

'What did you do?' he asked.

'Nothing!'

'You must have done something!'

It was drizzling but warm so we went around the corner for coffee and sat outside. Union officers and members were walking past and we didn't have much time to moan about things.

We were shell-shocked, Eugene even more than me. The charges against him were worse. I was charged with incompetence and dereliction of duty, but he was charged with having no integrity. His accusers, Bill Morris, Ray Collins and Margaret Prosser, are all in the House of Lords now – not a place known for its integrity! The arrogance astonishes me to this day. It was awful for Eugene, because if he knew something I'd done and said nothing, then he was complicit, whereas if he didn't know what I'd done he'd be incompetent. The real reason they went after him was that he would have defended me had he been left behind. At the time I was only fifty-four and although not yet eligible for a pension it was worse for Eugene because he was younger, with less service and small kids. I wondered what I'd done wrong. The *Six One News* on RTÉ featured the ATGWU and our suspension which, although true on one level, created the image that I was on the fiddle like all the other people who had been exposed. 'There's no smoke without fire' is the worst phrase in the English language.

The first person to ring me the following morning was Brendan Ogle, who had been secretary of the ILDA. 'Don't mind that, we'll fight it. It's only a collection of words.' He was full of optimism. 'No matter what happens you'll have a role, whether it's inside or outside the ATGWU.' That cheered me up for five minutes, until I got to thinking again about the hard practicalities of it all.

Bernard Browne also called, as did Albert McCready. Martin Walsh, who had been a shop steward in Packard and often argued against me, arrived at the house. The endless phone calls delayed my having to face up to the situation.

The Deputy General Secretary Margaret Prosser, who had been investigating the Irish region, never interviewed me. She spoke to me informally a couple of times but there was nothing on the record. It was the sloppiest piece of work, a template for how not to do a report. She never investigated the facts about ILDA members or the Cork Operative Butchers' Society joining us. She self-selected her interviewees, including people who had obtained jobs in the union by corrupt means. I didn't even see the report, let alone have a chance to respond to it, so I certainly didn't expect anything to happen at that stage, but Morris made a pre-emptive strike.

There was a prejudgement in Morris's letter setting up Prosser's investigation, because he stated: 'Each complaint in itself would not necessarily give cause for concern, however, when taken together there is a clear pattern.' No committee in the union in Ireland was ever interviewed, which is astonishing in a collective organization that makes collective decisions. A lot of the report was gossip about people forming opinions.

One of the accusations was that I ran the union in the South and allowed Eugene to run it in the North. That's not true, but even if it had been, what would be so terrible about that? For years, John Freeman ran the northern side of the union while Mattie Merrigan ran the southern side, and no one said a word. When I moved to Belfast, I certainly took advice from Eugene because, while I understood a lot about Northern Ireland, I wasn't so arrogant to believe that I knew everything. The allegations of administrative irregularities were fly shite, ridiculous from beginning to end, trivia going back years without a scintilla of evidence. None of it stands up. If any of it was serious it would have been brought up at the time, not years later.

Some years before my time in Belfast a female candidate, Joanna Carson, applied for a job with the union there and was asked her religion during the interview. She subsequently took a case against us. Eugene met her and told me he could settle it for £1000, so I instructed him to go ahead and the money was taken out of Irish region funds. I informed the TGWU legal director Fergus Whitty, who told me it was the best settlement he had ever seen: if a case like that came up in England there would be terrible publicity for the union. But Morris brought that up as a charge against me because I didn't write to him for permission.

A union administrator, Fiona Marshall, applied to become an officer in Belfast. John Freeman gave her the interview questions and answers beforehand and she got the job. Then she went for a promotion – but because this time he didn't give her the questions, she was unsuccessful. She took a case against the union and won, just before Freeman retired. Two other officers,

Bill Condit and Joe McCusker, testified that they were also given interview questions. This was done to damage Freeman, who didn't deserve that after leading the union so long in such difficult times. When I arrived in Belfast the legal officer there asked me, 'Are you the new man?' When I said I was, he went on, 'Well, God help you, Mr O'Reilly. He gave them jobs and look what they did to him. Imagine what they'll do to you!'

When the train drivers joined the ATGWU they filled in forms. I checked everything had been done, then sent those details to the office where they were entered into the computer. I don't know what happened to the papers after that – it wouldn't be the first time a few forms were lost in an office. The key thing is not whether an actual form is on file or not, but that someone's membership has been processed.

Jimmy Elsby took over the Irish region during my suspension. Under the 1975 Trade Union Act, to represent the union in Ireland you have to be resident on the island of Ireland. Elsby wasn't, and he even replaced me as a delegate to the ICTU. The Irish regional committee took a decision not to attend the ICTU conference because of our suspension, but the TGWU just brought over delegates. That was brought to the attention of the ICTU but the president Joe O'Toole said that was a matter for the TGWU, disregarding the ICTU's own constitution. I looked at the idea of injuncting the ICTU over that, but I didn't have the time because the conference was only a few days later. I didn't think they would leave a situation where the ATGWU would have no one on the ICTU executive.

A lawyer told me that what the union had done was completely illegal. Morris could bring me over to London and sack me over administrative matters, but in anything political or industrial he had no authority because that rested in Ireland. 'Great, you've convinced me. Now, will you ring Bill Morris and tell him?' My daughter, who was with me at the time, asked who was on the phone. I told her that he had represented people being pursued by the Criminal Assets Bureau, and she said, 'He must be really good, then. Drug dealers always buy the best.'

The Irish trade union movement could have written to Morris and told him that his internal disputes with me were his own affair but that he had no right to discipline me over any industrial or political matter. But they didn't. Des Geraghty was heckled over my treatment when he spoke at the May Day march in Dublin, and they were furious over that. They wanted to create the impression that they were on my side.

The TGWU's biennial delegate conference was on in Brighton at the same time as the ICTU's, and that was where the big battle took place. The English delegates put up a great fight for us and won the debate, but not the vote. They were told that if standing orders were overturned to discuss our case, delegates' expenses wouldn't be paid and they would all have to find their own way home. We nearly chinned them there, and we dominated the conference without even being there.

Anyone can run a union when they're in it, but it takes something else to swing decisions your way at executive meetings you're actually barred from attending. For that I am eternally grateful to the rank-and-file members who took great risks for me. It would have been easy for them to just pass a resolution supporting me and then move on to the next item on the agenda, but there was always somebody to keep pushing the issue.

I had good friends in the union: Albert McCready, who I spent ten years with on the executive, was unshakeable, Jimmy Kelly, Ted McKenna, people I knew as shop stewards stayed with me. I hadn't seen Ted for a while, and he rang me a couple of days after my suspension. As soon as I heard his voice I burst into tears, the only time I cried during that whole terrible time. Mary was extraordinarily angry about what Morris had done. She came with me to London for most of the hearings and took a tremendous interest in the case. I couldn't have done it without her.

One of the people I admired as a young Communist Party member was Georgi Dimitrov, the Bulgarian communist who was tried by the Nazis for the Reichstag fire. He was a courageous man, standing up in court to defy Hitler and the whole Reich, but in front of Stalin he crumbled. Why was that? I think it's about being understood by your own camp, and losing everything. Losing to Morris would have meant also losing my reputation, my honour, my sense of being in the Labour movement. Hitler couldn't do that to Dimitrov, but Stalin could. I'd never compare myself to Dimitrov, but that's the kind of idea with which I grappled at the time. Attacking the union felt counterintuitive. I reread Greaves' *Life and Times of James Connolly*, in which he says that 'revolutionaries dedicate themselves twice'. This was my second test: would I survive this hell and emerge unscathed?

Phil Flynn told me that if my case ended up in the Labour Court I could put him down as my representative – a huge endorsement from someone on the governing body of an institution such as this one.

Alex White, who was a barrister at the time, offered to take my case for nothing. I've been giving out about him as a government minister every day of the week since then, but he was good enough to offer me support back then. I would have gone down the legal route if the internal union procedures hadn't been successful.

Turlough O'Sullivan, the head of IBEC, told me the way I was being treated was awful. I had dealings with him – together we represented breweries in Dundalk in negotiations – and he would always mark your card rather than engage in class warfare.

While all this was going on, Kieran Mulvey was at a big industrial relations conference in England where Morris was present and lashed into him. Mulvey and I would never have been that close, but there was indignation, particularly over the fact that I was being brought over to London to be judged, as if I were Roger Casement.

Jimmy Kelly and Norman Cairns repeatedly raised our case during union elections. That strong, principled stand ensured that the union in Ireland was solidly behind us. Countless people stood with us under often difficult circumstances. Two shop stewards in Team Aer Lingus hadn't drawn their stewards' fees for years. The fee was tiny, but after ten or fifteen years it added up to a couple of thousand. They drew that money and split it between myself and Eugene. There were other supporters, too many to name, but I'm eternally in the debt of every one of them. A month later the charges against me arrived in a big fat file. I had to see for myself the totality of internal procedures within the TGWU before I could attack from the outside. I didn't think I could win the case inside the union, but power always trumps a good case.

I often thought of defying the ban on speaking to people but never did because it would have handed Morris victory on a plate. He would have suspended the whole process and sacked me. Then I would have brought him to an industrial tribunal and won a load of money but not reinstatement, because tribunals in Britain can't get you reinstated even if you win. I was tempted to speak out, because the idea of Bill Morris telling me that I couldn't speak at the Desmond Greaves School really stuck in my craw.

But I determined that the way to fight was the long war, with a change in the TGWU leadership coming up on the inside track. We considered a new union. I said I would join and even lead it, but only once the process in the ATGWU was exhausted. I met many officials in various unions who were prepared to jump ship if they could be sure of jobs in this new union.

Noel Murphy, a communist, was in favour of setting up the breakaway union, but Jimmy Kelly, who was in the Socialist Workers' Party, was hesitant and didn't think the time was right. Mick O'Riordan once told me after a meeting about this: 'I've heard everything now: a communist arguing to split the movement and a Trotskyite arguing to keep it together!' I was convinced I would end up in a new union because I didn't see how I could go back. But I did always say that I had to go through the procedures. We had no idea those procedures would take so long, but the union had to go on and Morris's schedule kept delaying things.

A union member has a right to go into a union office to pay contributions. It was authoritarian madness to deny me that and they soon backed down. I even conducted meetings there. The ban on speaking publicly lasted a long time, but by the magic of modern technology I was able to speak to everybody since RTÉ broadcast the interview I had recorded with Peter Cluskey on the morning of my suspension.

I did talk to journalists off the record, and found them much more amenable than I had on any other issue. Gene Kerrigan knocked down the case against us repeatedly in the *Sunday Independent*, which has a huge readership. Lots of people told me that reading his columns on the case convinced them we were right. He spoke at a meeting in Wynn's Hotel in my support and really came on board although he was very nervous. The *Would You Believe?* team also made a great documentary on me: you won't find many baptized atheists being profiled on RTÉ religious programmes!

Our reinstatement gave the union heart once again. Had we remained sacked, we would have become a millstone, with any complaint about an employee being countered with, 'Ah, but look what you did to O'Reilly and McGlone!' While in the end it did the union good, there's no doubt it damaged the image at the time. And it was expensive: there were reports and enquiries, people brought back and forth from England, you might be talking over a million pounds, not to mention the number of people who left the union over the matter.

Some of the ATGWU officials stood to gain from our misfortune. Somebody got my job and somebody got Eugene's; that's how they split people. And I made a big issue of my republicanism, which annoyed people, including Morris. My argument with him was that he had no authority over me. I maintained that taking part in his disciplinary process didn't confer any legitimacy on it, but I wasn't going to give him a walkover.

Kevin McCorry had been a leader of the civil rights movement in Northern Ireland, and had stood on the platform on Bloody Sunday in Derry when people were murdered. When Brendan Hodgers declined to represent me – how lucky I was that he did! – I saw Kevin at the Desmond Greaves School in September and casually asked if he would represent me in London. He asked how long it would take. 'Oh, it'll be over by Christmas,' I said. It was – Christmas three years later!

The coverage of Kevin doing the case couldn't have been better: 'Civil rights leader represents Irish official.' Eugene was represented by the Officers' National Committee, the shop stewards elected by TGWU officials themselves: Phil McNulty from Manchester, who was the secretary of that committee, and John Newe from London, the biggest region in the union. I would call John Newe a Cromwellian communist: not fanciful but blunt, direct in his language. The journey was interesting for him, because he had originally been a supporter of Morris, but gradually saw the mask slip. Phil McNulty was more diplomatic, but he faced down Morris. It's easy to represent workers against a big capitalist baron, but it takes special ability to represent people against your own union, and they played a magnificent role.

I never felt comfortable in the London office of the TGWU. Only people giving evidence were allowed in the room where the trial was taking place. Bill Morris sat there as the judge. Attached to his ear and keeping notes was Peter Rainier, truly the ugliest man who ever stood in shoe leather. He had come from an industrial relations background and had quite a right-wing record by all accounts, but was regarded as competent in the area of finance. Margaret Prosser was making the case for the prosecution.

On the first day Morris explained housekeeping matters and then went down to speak to Prosser. Kevin jumped to his feet and said: 'Can I remind you that you are the judge in this case, and you are speaking with the chief prosecutor?' Morris was aghast. When he regained his composure, he said that he was just discussing other union matters with the Deputy General Secretary. Kevin said: 'Well, I'm just putting you on notice. Make sure you don't talk about this case with her.' You could feel the coldness coming down like a cloak. This was the union I had grown up in, where problems were sorted out over a pint. But Kevin was perfectly right to put Morris to the cross.

There's a basic hotel near the union office, but we weren't put up there because mixing with officials would have been embarrassing. Instead, we stayed in a very expensive hotel round the corner, but of course we used to go down to the hotel by the union anyway. I always got to bed early if I was giving evidence the next day, but if we weren't performing, drinks and a sing-song would be had. When you're going through hell you have to break the tension. There were great nights during the trial, strange as that might sound, and gallows humour was in plentiful supply. Like Dickens said, it was the worst of times and the best of times. Something like that tests you and your belief system. We were arguing about the very soul of our union.

Early one morning Kevin showed me the copious trial notes he had taken for his summing up, but told me he didn't want to use them, he just wanted to talk ad lib. 'Kevin, I'm in your hands. Whatever you think is best, we'll do it,' I said.

He stood up and gave a speech, and I remember nothing of it except for one part. He told Morris that he had always been an admirer of the TGWU: its democracy, its leadership and its policies had always appealed to him. 'I have seen people murdered for their political views,' he said, 'but I have seldom seen such naked hatred as you have shown towards these two men. You're a disgrace to your office.' Morris was thoroughly shaken. Unsurprisingly, myself and Eugene were dismissed.

Our great forum for communication was the smoking room. Morris's secretary used to smoke like a trooper, and she told us he had warned her not to use the union's computers to look at the website we had set up on the case. I asked her what she was going to do about that, and she just said: 'Well, I've rejoined my local library.' They banned officials throughout the union looking at the website, which was stupid, because it guaranteed that people *would* look at it.

We made sure to talk to people in the union – not necessarily about the case, but just talking, because people always try to dehumanize you when they're doing you in. One day Eugene and I found ourselves in the lift in Transport House in London with the three members of the executive who were trying our case. I looked at them and said: 'Tell the truth now and shame the devil. If the three of you were sacked, who would you want representing you: me and Eugene, or Bill and Collins?' They burst out laughing and it broke the ice.

While our appeal was pending, the union wrote to say I had to vacate my house in Belfast for which they were helping to pay. I was lucky I had the house in Dublin, but it shows the level of vindictiveness and reminded me of the old miners and railworkers who had tied houses belonging to their employer. It was a sad reflection on what I always thought was a decent, humane and ethical organization – and 99 per cent of the time, that's what the TGWU was. James Klugman used to say that the saddest sentence in *The Ragged Trousered Philanthropists* is 'Human nature's human nature and you can't get away from it.' As a socialist you have to be optimistic about the possibilities of human nature and a union should be in the forefront when it comes to treating people decently. And decency, when it gets mixed up in a power struggle, can go right out the window.

At the start of the appeal I'd asked the chairman what the outcome would be. 'Of course, I don't know what the outcome is,' he said. 'We're here to investigate that.'

I held up the letter. 'Well, the union administration do, because they've told me to leave my home.' They were within their rights, because pending the appeal I was no longer an employee, but they were so bamboozled that proceedings were adjourned and the letter was withdrawn.

I was surprised by Brendan Hodgers, who had been a very good shop steward in Echo in Dundalk in my time there. We were great friends. I had given him books by Connolly, supported him when his wife died, helped him get a job in the union. When people told me Brendan was going for my job, I refused to believe them and went to see him in Dundalk. 'People tell me you're going for my job, but I know you're not.'

'Ah, I have to go for it. If I don't, Condit could get it,' he replied sheepishly.

'No,' I said, 'if you go for it, you'll be Condit.' I walked out.

He never gave me an explanation. I wrote a regular regional secretary's report, which I would hand out to every member of the regional committee at meetings, without recognizing him in his regional secretary's job. Hodgers never stopped me, even though it was illegal. In one of the reports I lifted something that Bernard Browne had written on the case: 'From Judas to Carey to Stakeknife and all those in between, those who betray their friends will never be trusted by anybody.' He should have given me a dig in the mouth for that because it was a savage thing to say, but I meant it and used my words carefully, knowing that the references to informers wouldn't be missed by someone with his republican views. The other officers in Belfast were fantastic. In many ways they had it worse, because I was outside while they were inside getting battered by bureaucracy.

When Prosser resigned as Deputy General Secretary in 2002 Tony Woodley won the election to succeed her hands down, which changed everything. During my suspension period a meeting took place between Tony Woodley, Jack Adams, Barry Camfield and John Aiken. Tony Woodley (who later became general secretary) indicated that he would consider not running for the position if myself and Eugene McGlone were reinstated. Astonishingly, they did not take up this offer. Barry Camfield stood for the position of general secretary, along with Tony Woodley and others, and Tony topped the poll. He said he would reinstate myself and Eugene as part of his election pledge. This was easier said than done because the people who had got our positions had got them lawfully.

Dawn Stuart won the election to lead the local authorities trade group, an unusual position for a member from Northern Ireland where we have very few people in local authorities. Our supporters almost won a majority on the TGWU executive. There was a section of the Left on the executive who refused to support us: they might have agreed we were badly done by, but thought the Left's influence would be stronger if they were with the General Secretary. That's a dangerous view, which can lead to lost purpose and principle.

Eugene called to say that the TGWU officials were threatening to go on strike in our support. Morris made it clear that if that happened, he would pass the picket and open up the union offices himself, threatening us with all the legal powers that Thatcherism had bestowed upon employers. I didn't believe Eugene at first. Mick O'Riordan said, 'That's like the cardinals voting against the Pope. I'm telling you now, Morris is fucked. You'll be back.'

Officers in London weren't voting to support me because they knew me; very few of them did. They were voting against Morris, against intolerance, because they knew the same thing could happen to them. And they were right. Officials have to obey instructions, but they have to make decisions on their feet all the time. If you can find yourself up on a charge for the slightest administrative error, what kind of a union is that? Everyone would be careful, no one would ever make a mistake, and we'd all go down the tubes together. Making officials fearful would ruin a union, particularly one like the TGWU, which is used to a very robust culture.

The Irish executive of the union requested a review of the case, which was carried out by John Hendy, the famous QC. I had an argument with Tony over this because I wanted John Stalker to do the review: Tony believed that had Stalker done the review, he would have become the story rather than the issue at hand.

I always felt that the mastermind behind all this thinking was Len McCluskey. In any event, the Hendy report totally vindicated us. It was accepted by the General Executive Council and we got our jobs back and were to be regarded as having no broken service (meaning I had remained regional secretary throughout my suspension period).

Morris's control of the union executive was dependent on the chairman's casting vote, and at the next election that chairman lost his seat over that to Tom Cashman, an Irish busman and supporter. The implications for the TGWU and the wider trade union movement were huge. The bureaucracy in Ireland were astonished that I came back. I was a bit flabbergasted myself.

We were brought back on the same pay but debarred from applying for our old jobs. This was done to placate Morris, who had suffered a terrible defeat. John Newe and Phil McNulty wrote to say that we had gone as far as we could in this battle and now we should go back to work; the officials would take up the fight to get us back in our positions. To be fair, they did take it up and the Irish regional committee demanded an inquiry, which then recommended our full reinstatement.

I was barred from applying for my old job, but did so anyway, just to keep them under pressure. In the meantime I was doing very little work, although it was fascinating to be at the coalface in Belfast. I remember dealing with the case of a Protestant woman working for Seán Graham, the bookies, who had been moved to their Falls Road shop. She came in to me and said, 'I could be murdered up there.' Personally, I don't think she was in any danger on the Falls Road, but it wasn't my place to decide that for her. I asked her what she wanted me to do, and she said: 'Come along and stand with me and tell them I want to be moved.' I told her I'd have no problem doing that, and she said: 'Oh, I know you'll have no problem with it. Aren't you a union man?' I thought that was great, even though it was only a simple thing. The reputation of the union in Belfast meant that this Protestant woman knew that an official like me, presumably a Catholic with my Dublin accent, would stand by her. She had to work another few days on the Falls and was then quietly allowed to move.

An atmosphere of fear was starting to develop in the union under Bill Morris, and our case was his Waterloo. When he eventually retired from the union very few people went to his leaving party. That was sad because being the first black union leader was a big deal. He had lived through tough times as a black man in Britain but he had become a part of the British establishment. Morris's father had been in the Jamaican police and belonged to the generation that admired the British empire. Someone who worked with him once told me that Morris was one of those people who think Belfast is wonderful because you can get a train from there to Ireland!

No other TGWU General Secretary would have done what Morris did, and he wouldn't have done it without being sure that he was going to win. But it damaged his capacity to influence who would follow him, because when his successor was being elected Elsby got the lowest vote out of four. I once told Elsby: 'Like a lot of people who have come over here from Britain, you'll think you'll make a name for yourself for taking our heads off, but I predict now that you'll sink in an Irish bog.' And it did destroy him.

An unofficial meeting of the TGWU took place during the election of a new General Secretary, despite being banned by the leadership. People gave up their Sunday, sometimes driving down from Edinburgh or Aberdeen – a long way when your boss is refusing to pay your expenses. It was a terrific turnout. I told them: 'Jimmy Elsby is standing in this election and says he agrees with Morris that we should be sacked: that's clear. Tony Woodley says that he'll take us back: that's clear. The rest are saying they want further investigation, enquiries and so on: that's not clear, and whatever else those candidates are, they're not leaders.' The place was torn down with applause, and I knew then Woodley was in.

The only time I talked to Hodgers again was when Woodley met us at Liverpool airport just before getting on a plane to Beijing. Anyone else would take the full day for something like that, but Tony Woodley is the kind of person who would solve the Irish question in a two-hour stopover between Liverpool and China. We went for a coffee. Woodley started by saying, in his thick Scouse accent, 'Here we are, three lads, all victims of Irish history.' Hodgers might think he was the regional secretary, but he wasn't. If he had to sack him, he would. Hodgers might take a legal case and he might win a big bag of money, but if he moved sideways, he could keep the same pay. One way or another, I was returning as regional secretary and O'Reilly and McGlone would also be reinstated. 'I'm off to China now, so you've got five minutes to tell me what you want to do.' I went back.

The TGWU was a powerful union with big resources, a great place to work. On the streets of Belfast and threatened with dismissal, I asked myself whether it had all been an illusion and concluded that the good experiences were all true – but then so were the bad ones. Justice prevailed in the end, but it could have gone the other way.

SEVENTEEN

*At a certain stage of development, the material productive forces of
society come into conflict with the existing relations of production
... Then begins an era of social revolution.*

Karl Marx

The first ICTU conference I attended after returning to the job was in
Belfast. I was delighted when John Freeman turned up to stand at the door
and shake my hand. He was putting two fingers up to the executive, but
luckily some of the worst of the ICTU had left by the time I came back.

There was an attempt to close down ATGWU offices in a rationalization
plan. Union membership was growing by about 7 per cent a year, which
wasn't happening in many other TGWU regions. We were standing up for
something different in trade union terms. As Shaw said, if there are two
people exactly alike there's no need for one of them, and that's also true
of organizations. I've always believed there should be at least two unions
in the world: one for everybody, and the other for everybody else. There

are dangers in having just one. Challenges, argumentation, a little bit of competition are good things. It amazes me how in 1994 the unions could sign up to something called the Programme for Competitiveness and Work but then demand a monopoly in their own movement.

I was in favour of the merger that created Unite. In Ireland, the biggest union we were dealing with was the radical Manufacturing Science and Finance union. The other one was Amicus, which was particularly big in the North. The picture in Britain was more complicated: one of the things I worry about in the new structure is that the officials seem to be less under the control of branches than they used to be. On the other hand, there are good things to be said in favour of the merged union. Ireland's autonomy within Unite is completely protected, but that's got very little to do with its structures or personalities. After what happened to us, any General Secretary in London might sack any regional secretary but never an Irish secretary. I dread to see what happens if we get some right-wing bastard running the union in Ireland! But it'll be a long day before anyone goes for an Irish official again. That lesson has been truly learned.

The union borrowed ideas from America and Australia, essentially a model of organizing people on an industrial basis. I met Andy Stern, president of the Service Employees International Union in the US, who quoted a cleaner in New York whose official asked her what he could do about her wages. She replied: 'My wages are fine. What you need to do is deal with the competition who are trying to take my job. Get them my wages.' You try to organize the whole sector. You need to get across the idea that members pay the union not just to service them personally – which they're fully entitled to, of course – but to organize other workers who aren't in the union yet. It requires much more self-organization by members while resources are put into organizers concentrating on the rest of the industry. That's the theory, anyway. It needs a debate within the union over resources, and it doesn't always pay off, but all the research shows that the main reason people don't join a union is that they were never asked.

We need to engender a collectivist culture again. That's what transforms the world. Unions are the core organizations of working people but they need to be better managed. You won't create socialist parties, challenge the system or realign politics if you don't organize people on the shop floor. 'Public enterprise' is a phrase that trips easily off the lips of the Left, but the biggest enemy of enterprise is actually the banks, who are just putting money into making money and discouraging people who want to make *things*.

When I represented bank managers I wanted them to have a say in the direction the bank was taking. But they were told very firmly that the bank was run by the shareholders. I was sitting in the office one day when a well-dressed, well-spoken man in his early sixties came in. He talked for a few moments, then burst into tears. I wasn't really equipped to deal with that, but asked him what was wrong, 'I've been taken into a romper room and told to forget everything I ever learned about banking. They're not interested any more in the proper balance between investment and outflow. They told me to forget about all that, that Anglo Irish were successful and I need to follow them, or else.' They had given him targets, and it was implied that if he didn't reach them, he could be disciplined.

'We'll get the workforce behind you. They'll support you,' I told him. We held a ballot and decided that if anyone was disciplined over a target we would defend them with industrial action. The bank took out an injunction, naming the whole committee. Being named was for me a badge of honour, but the bank workers – who might want to work in other institutions – were fearful, so I persuaded the bank to make the injunction just against me.

I kept up the campaign. The bank agreed to let the court case drop and we started negotiating. It was around the time the Criminal Assets Bureau raided Phil Flynn when he had worked as a mediator in bank negotiations. When mediators were being discussed this time, I said, 'I propose Phil Flynn.'

'Oh, we couldn't have Phil Flynn!' they cried.

'Why?'

I knew they couldn't say why – allegations about him were flying around, but they couldn't say anything officially.

'Well, let's go to the Labour Court. I'll argue why we should have Phil Flynn, and you can argue why we shouldn't. If you won't tell me your reasons, maybe you'll tell the chairman of the Labour Court and put it on the record.'

I knew I had the fuckers against the wall. All my own people in the ATGWU were with me. We decided there would be three adjudicators: the chairman of the Labour Court, Phil Flynn and John Behan, who had mutilated the unions in Team Aer Lingus. Then I rang Phil Flynn, who was a kind of revolutionary member of the establishment. I had no idea whether he would do it or not. I said, 'First of all, if everything they're saying about you in the press is absolutely correct, you've gone up in my estimation. Secondly, I'm after nominating you as an adjudicator. Don't fucking say no! You can't!'

He did it, and I won the thing.

It's an interesting snapshot of banking culture. We were arguing for solid banking ethics, that people's talents should be used. They were saying, 'Fuck that overboard! Look at Anglo Irish. Follow the money!' These people were reducing trained, professional bankers to salesmen and destroying Ireland in the process. And I see no evidence that anything has been learned from this.

Sinn Féin didn't have enough councillors to elect anyone in the 2007 Senate election. They decided to do a deal with Labour to help elect Labour people on bigger panels, in return for Labour giving them the votes they needed to get Sinn Féin people elected on smaller panels. I said that I would run for one of the smaller panels. Sinn Féin votes wouldn't be enough to get me elected, but if I could gather votes from elsewhere I'd be in. I met a variety of Sinn Féin people – Mitchel McLaughlin in Stormont, Pat Doherty in Dublin – and went off to find the other votes.

The experience was quite funny. Tony Gregory said: 'What are you ringing me for? Ring other people and get their votes. Of course I'm voting for you, who else would I vote for?' He was very straightforward, but others insisted I meet them, which is fair enough. One of the most interesting people I met was Ming Flanagan, with whom I spent a couple of hours and who promised me his vote. I gave people a copy of the *Would You Believe?* documentary – or 'The Greatest Story Ever Told' as I was starting to call it – although that may have put some people off me.

Sinn Féin were hesitant about me meeting their councillors directly instead of going through the party leadership, but I was always assured that the votes were there. A night or two before the end Sinn Féin called to tell me I'd only be getting a certain number of their votes. I needed all their votes to get in, but they had done a deal with Labour and others. I hit the roof – not because I had any entitlement to Sinn Féin's votes, I had none – but because they had made an arrangement.

I wrote a long letter to Gerry Adams in which I said, among other things, that making arrangements with people and then breaking them was no way to advance his party. I met him on the Falls Road. Our exchange was frank but not acrimonious. He didn't want to get into an argument over what did or didn't happen, but he pointed out that he had never endorsed the agreement. I get the impression that very little goes on in Sinn Féin he doesn't know about. I admire him, especially for the way he has succeeded in bringing more military republicans with him than any other republican leader.

We shook hands and I told him a story I had heard from Johnny Nolan. The Communist Party wanted something raised in the Dáil, and Johnny was sent up to discuss it with Roddy Connolly, who had by then become a Labour TD in Louth. When Johnny came back, he was asked how he got on. 'I didn't even raise the matter,' he said. 'He was sitting there with a big tome on parliamentary procedure open in front of him on the table. I concluded that it was a waste of time to ask someone like that anything to do with revolutionary activity.'

As Lenin said about the Duma in Tsarist Russia, sometimes you have to go into a pigsty to clean things up. I decided to run for vice presidency of the ICTU in 2007. The contest is always for the vice presidency, and the vice president then goes on to become president. Jerry Shanahan also decided to run, although we were then in the process of a merger with his union Amicus. I told him that under no circumstances would I withdraw from the election, that I would stand against him if necessary. I met Jack O'Connor of SIPTU, who told me that I would have the SIPTU vote if Shanahan withdrew. It seemed too good to be true. I didn't stand for the ICTU executive, which is like getting on the high wire without a net: if I didn't get the vice presidency, I'd have nothing. But it was a deliberate move, since anyone running against me would be doing so to eliminate me from Congress.

Jerry Shanahan was persuaded to withdraw. Then O'Connor said he'd be unable to give me his union's vote as promised. I asked him why. 'I can't tell you, but there are people who have stopped me doing it.' I told him he shouldn't be coming to me complaining about the big boys in the school yard telling him what he could and couldn't do. He begged me to run for the executive, saying he would vote for me and propose me for this committee and that, but I refused. He himself stood for the vice presidency, and I lost.

I would have been delighted to serve as president of Congress, and I'm the only ATGWU leader who never did, but that's the way it worked out. Jack did not want to do what he did. He wanted to honour his arrangement with me and it hurt him not to. The people who were delighted when Morris sacked me and disgusted when I got back determined the way events turned out. I may well have done something to offend them, but it would have been better for us to have it out face to face.

Being a union official is challenging, rewarding and enjoyable. Sometimes it's a pain in the arse, like any job, but you have to have an empathy for workers, a belief in them and in yourselves. You have no boss but your members.

My management style – telling people what the difficulties were, refusing to meet management behind their back, leading but always abiding by the members' decision – made my life easier. Most people I knew weren't born with a silver spoon in their mouth. I always believed in building up shop stewards, educating and influencing them politically; not necessarily to join anything, but to think about themselves and their status in life.

By 2008 I'd decided it was time to leave. I wanted to do other things: get an education, reconnect with friends, take life a bit easier and become an activist again. Someone else needed to step in after the merger, and so I left a couple of years early. I didn't want to hang around, waiting for my demise. Jimmy Kelly replaced me as regional secretary. He came straight in from the shop floor, which was unusual but not unprecedented. In some other unions that wouldn't happen, and even people from the lower bureaucracy have to serve their time moving up slowly through the ranks. We do have to measure our behaviour against what we've done before, but it's very unimaginative to do everything according to precedent, which makes us like the civil service instead of a trade union. Bernard Browne told me about a leader in the WUI who said when he left, in all sincerity: 'As a follower of Larkin I'm delighted to say that I've left this union exactly as I found it.' Bernard added: 'If Larkin had left his union exactly as he found it, he would have achieved nothing.'

I was surprised at the extent of the recession at the end of 2008. The first part of the Celtic Tiger was relatively healthy in capitalistic terms – we weren't creating an egalitarian or democratic society, but we were producing and exporting successfully on our own terms. But the second part was a disaster. We put money into property because it was quick and easy and looked good.

Karl Marx said that you don't go from one phase of history to another except when an existing form of organization becomes a fetter on the productive forces – and under modern capitalism finance is becoming a fetter on production. The capitalism of my childhood was dominated by the Fords and the Chryslers and engineering companies, but now it's all about the hedge funds. But at least the older guys made money by creating things, whereas these people make money by manipulating other money.

Do the Left then champion the cause of capitalists who actually make things as opposed to finance capital? And if we do, what concessions do we give them?

The banks are so dominant that they're too big to fail, and states won't countenance the idea of taking them over and running them democratically. The bankers were able to bamboozle Brian Cowen and Brian Lenihan in 2008, who gave them the guarantees they needed: these bankers were effectively running the country at that moment, which was a huge threat to democracy.

The lesson of the collapse is to find models of democracy that work and deepen people's participation and involvement. We can't interfere with the market dictating the big economic decisions, but that's a challenge we can meet, bringing people with us towards a more democratic and egalitarian society. In the first experiment at building socialism in the world the Left moved away from democracy under Stalin in the Soviet Union. But if there's one lesson to be learned from the twentieth century, it's that you can't construct any kind of a society that serves people rather than profit without democracy. Socialism now is about the extension of democracy.

The ICTU did get an agreement that there would be no compulsory redundancies in the public sector and that pay cuts would eventually be restored, but they didn't identify with people outside the movement who were suffering from the recession. Instead, they put their hopes in Labour, which was a catastrophic mistake. Labour did achieve some things from being in government, but not in proportion to what could have been achieved through the building of a mass movement and a Left government.

The self-confidence of shop stewards has been hugely weakened. When the crisis struck, people were asking what 'the union' was going to do; as if it were something outside themselves. I never heard that in the car industry: workers decided what they were going to do and then made the union follow. We had the self-confidence to stop the production process. That's largely gone, partly the result of national wage agreements. Strong centralized leadership from the top of the trade union movement was needed in that crisis. With fear all around, the centre becomes important, but instead it was every man for himself.

Nowadays many trade union leaders can't speak at demonstrations in Dublin for the sheer anger of workers who feel the unions have let them down. We need to build a new relationship with those people, not talk down to them. The unions in the Right2Water campaign have shown an imaginative approach, and we need more political thinking like that.

It was absolutely fantastic going back to education after I retired. I got on famously with a number of American ex-servicemen in the class, as well as a couple of nuns. When I went to Trinity College for the first time I got a little bit tearful thinking about my parents, because although I wasn't born that far from Trinity, in social terms it was a million miles away. I wrote my thesis on Irish neutrality, a subject I knew nothing about. I wanted a challenge.

I was once ambiguous about de Valera's policy of neutrality, but now believe it was the only thing he could have done. It was the greatest expression of Irish independence since the founding of the state. His fancy footwork kept the state out of the war, which was quite an achievement. Nobody believes in Irish neutrality as a project anymore, but neutrality is still on people's minds – and a political party which makes an issue of preserving neutrality would find a lot of support.

I acted as a workers' representative on the employment appeals tribunal. At the beginning of the recession I saw loads of building workers coming up, many of them immigrants, and their employer was just the man next to them who owned the wheelbarrow. It was effectively self-employment, and in many cases they were entitled to nothing.

I was president of the Trades Council for the centenary of the 1913 lockout and spoke at the SIPTU conference as a fraternal delegate. You should always have two-day conferences on the Left: the first day for people to exhaust themselves beating one another up until their anger has dissipated, and the second to move things forward. We had huge demonstrations – about 25,000 people on one of the first against the cutbacks – and we've brought a host of community groups in with us.

Being on the Trades Council has brought me back into contact with some of the people I started out with. Sam Nolan is still secretary and recently made his fiftieth speech at a May Day rally. He's in his eighties now but sharper than most people I know.

The Left has great potential, but really has to go back to old ideas and apply them to new circumstances. Marx's society run by workers is the way forward. Trotsky said socialism without democracy is like life without air: it has to be about expanding democracy and participation, otherwise it won't work. Political realignment on the Left will also involve realignment on the Right, perhaps Fine Gael and Fianna Fáil being in government together, or maybe Fine Gael on their own. Perhaps an openly right-wing government would be an unmitigated disaster, but that preaches our own impotence. We still have tens of thousands of people organized in unions, including people who work directly for the government.

Realignments in Irish politics have traditionally taken place over the national question: from the Parliamentary Party to Sinn Féin in 1918, from Cumann na nGaedheal to Fianna Fáil in 1932. What we've had since is a slow evolution of Fianna Fáil towards Fine Gael, with Labour occasionally going in with one of them. The Soviet Union was condemned as a one-party state, but in Ireland we've had a one-policy state. The fundamental policies of the two parties have been pretty much identical since the mid-1950s, bar the odd tax cut here or there. This has become even more obvious since the 2016 election with a minority government based on cooperation between Fianna Fáil and Fine Gael.

Now it's possible to take a different direction, to bring about a fundamental change in the political culture. Labour could have led that, but instead we have the worst of all worlds with Sinn Féin, a radical nationalist party, although it has many socialists and good people in it. They won't have the same conviction around social issues as they did over the national question. Taking up arms against the state is a revolutionary act but nationalism is a force capable of ploughing any furrow. As Lenin said, 'Don't paint nationalism red,' although that doesn't mean you shouldn't try and push nationalists to the Left. They may end up like de Valera or not, and it's up to us to influence that.

Sinn Féin aren't engaged with the trade union movement in the sense of their members being involved on the ground. Even the Far Left and people who call themselves Marxists have been very bad there. They can describe the trade unions and prescribe for them, but they haven't developed people with stature, an ability to negotiate and a following in the unions. Unless you do that on a big scale you're not going to change Ireland.

Perhaps a Labour–Fine Gael government would have been different had Labour been on its own, but looking around Europe that doesn't seem to be true. Unlike its counterparts in Europe, the Irish Labour Party has never been a colonial party, but its thinking is very weak. The Left in Europe is attempting to push its agenda while staying in the euro, and we'll see whether that works out. I take the view that we would be better off outside the euro, but that would be very difficult to implement.

The trade union movement is largely seen as not fit for purpose, but in terms of policy that is changing, with unions arguing that economic recovery has to be based on wage increases. That's a new tune, which hasn't been heard from Congress for decades, but I'm glad they're playing it. There are signs of hope within the movement.

I've spent my life trying to be a good communist, even though for most of that time I wasn't paying any party dues. Even during my years in the Labour Party I always tried to act like a communist. The world is a big place – we all have our own little garden to put in order; pulling out weeds and planting things and hoping that it'll all work out all right. But the more people who help during the process, the better. I owe everything to joining the Communist Party back in the 1960s. I know all the shortcomings of communism but I still retain a faith in Marxism and a fundamental belief in the self-organization of workers, which is the only thing that can change the world.

Acknowledgments

I ask myself the question of whether it is worthwhile telling the story of my life and not the story of the thousands of other people I worked with and fought employers for over the years. I'm sure many of them have a similar story to mine, but workers like us rarely go to print – our stories are usually told by others. I showed this book to an academic comrade of mine Helena Sheen and she made a comment that I find very gratifying: 'It's not an "I" book.' I'm very happy about that. It is enough to fill in a small part of the jigsaw where my life and the lives of likeminded people intersected with Irish history and trade unionism in Britain and Ireland. To me, this is worth exploring.

This book is dedicated to my wife, Mary, our two daughters, Louise and Suzanne, my grandchildren, Dyllen, Caitlin, Eoghan and Ciara, and my great-grandson, Tadgh. It is also dedicated to my sister Terry and my sister Anna (deceased), and to my oldest friend and comrade, Bernard (deceased). Also, Eugene McGlone who endured the dismissals with me and stood with me in dark days until we won our victory – thank you.

To the officers, staff, and rank-and-file members of the TGWU who supported and sustained us in our hour of need and who were indispensable in the battle – thank you, too.

I also want to acknowledge our representatives Kevin McCorry, Phil McNulty and John Newe, who displayed outstanding tenacity throughout the whole proceedings.

To all my friends and comrades who worked ceaselessly and never wavered in the battle, a big thank you.

Thank you is also due to Tony Woodley and Len McCluskey for their courage, tenacity and ingenuity that helped so many.

I wish to acknowledge the help of Francy Devine of the Irish Labour History Society, who was the first to suggest that I undertake this memoir; Aindrias O Cathasaigh, who spent hours recording me and typing it up; to Tony Boucher, John Montgomery and Eddie Glackin, who read the book and encouraged me to publish it; and also Helena Sheehan and Sam Nolan for reading the book and commenting on it. Thank you, as well, to my editor, Djinn von Noorden, whose work is much appreciated. Any shortcomings in the book are my own.

To Unite Regional Secretary Jackie Pollock, retired Regional Secretary Jimmy Kelly, and Len McCluskey, who have encouraged and supported this book.

Also a big thanks to Alex Klemm for her invaluable suggestions and editing, and to my publisher, the Lilliput Press.

Appendix 1

CONNOLLY YOUTH MOVEMENT

SIR,—Your article of July 30th on the meeting of the Connolly Youth Movement pointed out that one of the aims of the Connolly Youth Movement was to destroy the parliamentary system. This is a distortion of the facts. What the speaker intended to convey was the fault between the Parliamentary Labour Party and the rank and file members. The Connolly Youth Movement deplores the gulf as it is not in the interest of genuine democracy. As a Socialist organisation we are not indifferent to the type of government of our country. Limited as capitalist democracy is we realised that parliament, trade-union rights and democratic elections are not gifts from God but the products of the struggle of generations of working class, national and democratic elements of our people.

The threat to democracy does not come from the Connolly Youth Movement or any other section of the Irish Labour movement, but from Fianna Fail Government and monopoly interests in our country that have reduced the parliament to a farce, and threatened our trade-union rights.

It is modern monopoly capitalism that is proving itself incompatible with democracy. The fight to defend and extend democracy does come from the struggle for socialism. Socialism and democracy are two sides of the same coin, one being incomplete without the other.—Yours, etc.,

MICHAEL O'REILLY.
Chairman.
Connolly Youth movement,
37 Pembroke Lane,
Dublin 4.

CONFIDENTIAL
S.1/2/12.
Dublin Castle.

Chief Supt.,
S.B. Unit.

Detective Branch,
S.B. Unit,

22/11/'67.

Connolly Youth Movement.

Reference above I wish to report an executive committee meeting of the Connolly Youth was held in 37 Pembroke Lane, Ballsbridge on Sunday 19/11/'67.

Bernard Brown, 44 Kildonan Road, Finglas acted as Chairman and the speaker was Liam Mulready, 17 Nth Leinster St, Phibsboro who stated that he had met Declan Bree, 4 John Street, Sligo and introduced him to Johnny Nolan at the book shop, 16a Pearse Street. Declan Bree informed him that approximately 15 youths were interested in the Connolly Youth Movement in Sligo and on his return to Sligo he brought copies of Connolly and Marxist writings. Delegates from the executive of the Connolly Youth will travel at a later date to meet the interested youths.

A Connolly Youth Movement public meeting will be held in Limerick, but no date has been fixed, a public address system will be used.

The Ballyfermot group of the Connolly Youth are causing concern to the executive committee. They are making demands for £6 to £8 for a duplicating machine and printing paper. They have elected a Branch Secretary and Treasurer and they aim to infiltrate as many committees in the Ballyfermot area as possible. It was decided by the executive committee to investigate the activities of this group.

The financial report was read by Thomas Duff, 505 Howth Road, Raheny who stated that they now had £21-0-0 and he expected to get £7 for loaning the film on Vietnam to student [*sic*]. It had cost £8 to have the film flown from London and Mrs. Frank Edwards, 32 Richmond Grove, Monkstown who was visiting London had bought it back.

The following attended :—

1) Liam Mulready, 17 Nth Leinster St, Phibsboro.
2) Bernard Brown, 44 Kildonan Road, Finglas.
3) Sean Edwards, 32 Richmond Grove, Monkstown.
4) Eric Fleming, 73 Tolka Road, Ballybough.
5) Michael O'Reilly, 453 Landen Road, Ballyfermot
6) Thomas Duff, 505 Howth Road, Raheny.
7) Bernard Rogers, 83 Merchant Road, East Wall.

Appendix 2

Taken from the author's opening statement to the TGWU disciplinary hearing, November 2001:

I have spent thirty-nine years as an active member of the union. There is a small period of broken service due to unemployment. I have completed twenty-three years as a full-time officer of the ATGWU. I am the second-longest-serving Irish officer in the Irish region. This process that I am being subjected to is not legitimate as far as I am concerned, nor does my attendance here today convey any legitimation on this process and these procedures. These procedures, which I am being subjected to, are lacking insofar as they do not have the consent of those whom they apply to. No ballot of the officers has taken place to legitimate this process. There is also a difficulty in respect of the role of the General Secretary, Brother Bill Morris, and the Deputy General Secretary, Sister Margaret Prosser.

Prejudgement and procedures

The Central Office through the General Secretary Bill Morris, sets out, in a letter dated 5 December 2000 to Margaret Prosser, terms of reference: 'Each complaint in itself would not necessarily give cause for concern, however, when taken together there is a clear pattern relating to both the issues and the individuals involved.' This is clearly a prejudgement. It alleges 'there is a clear pattern'. In the circumstances where Margaret Prosser is a subordinate officer to the General Secretary, this is a prejudicial way to carry out an investigation. It undermines the credibility of the investigation, and therefore its capability of coming to fair conclusions.

I have in my possession correspondence from Brother Ray Sherlock, a former General Executive Council member, dated 13.08.01, the contents of which are supported by Brother John Ennis, another former executive member. This correspondence describes a meeting, which took place between Brother Sherlock and the Region 5 Regional Secretary Brother Jim Hunt in the week prior to my appointment as the Irish Regional Secretary. He describes how the three executive members would have a meeting with the Regional Secretary over the agenda for the Executive Council in the following week. The appointment of a new Irish Regional Secretary was on the agenda, and Brother Sherlock states that the Regional Secretary said to him during this meeting: 'You will be aware that Bill Morris, Margaret Prosser and Ray Collins don't want O'Reilly as Regional Secretary and would prefer you to support Liam McBrinn.' Brother Sherlock then goes on to describe the threats that were made to Brother John Ennis if he were to vote for me.

This statement, together with the prejudgement in the letter to Sister Prosser, clearly establishes that it is unfair for Bill Morris to act as a judge in these matters, and I am therefore calling upon him to step aside as a judge in this case. I also believe that it was unfair to ask Margaret Prosser to carry out this investigation because of the prejudgement made by the General Secretary in his letter to her and because of the prejudicial view she expressed about me (please refer to letter from Ray Sherlock).

On p. 12 (and various other pages) of the bundle, Sister Prosser refers to interviews that were conducted. She mentions that she interviewed me. I wish to state categorically that no such interview with me took place, nor was I asked, as other interviewees were, to sign off on the documentation. I believe that this totally prejudices the situation against me: an investigation is carried out into the Region, and I was ignored. As the most senior officer in the Region, the very least I expected was a formal interview, and I am now requesting that all references to this 'interview' be deleted from this document, and that the document is therefore set aside and a formal interview with me takes place. There are many instances in this report where Sister Prosser refers to me: e.g. on p. 24 of the bundle she accuses me of carelessness and disinterest in respect of managing the affairs of the region. How could she come to these conclusions without having interviewed me? Instead she went to a self-selecting group of people such as Joe McCusker, Fiona Marshall and Billy Condit, whose record in the union is well known, and Margaret herself is aware that they engaged in unfair practices to get their jobs (which is on record in a tribunal finding). I feel, as the most senior officer in Ireland, it was grossly unfair to treat me in this way.

It is also interesting that none of the constitutional committees, the officers; committee or the staff committee were asked to comment on any aspect of this report, notwithstanding the fact that this report touches upon industrial and polit- ical matters. It is astonishing that the views of the committees in Ireland set up to deal with such matters were not consulted. This is contrary to the constitution of the ICTU, it is contrary to the laws governing unions in Ireland, it is contrary to a request made by the Irish regional committee which, on 15 December 2000, met in emergency session and requested a meeting with the chairman of the Executive Council and the General Secretary Brother Morris and requested that they be allowed investigate all of these matters. In effect the regional administration, the regional committee and all the constitutional committees in Ireland have been ignored in this investigation.

This action places the union in conflict with section 75 of the Irish Trade Union Act and with the constitution of Congress, and shows a complete lack of understanding of the Irish membership. Those who initiated this report appear to believe that Ireland is like any other region of the union. This, of course, was a view which was famously put forward by Margaret Thatcher to John Hume when she said that Northern Ireland was as British as Finchley. This is not a view that was taken historically in Ireland. I want to quote a former member of the General Executive Council, Brother Andy Holmes. Speaking at the reunification congress at the foundation of the ICTU in the early sixties he said '... on the new constitution of Congress, which established the right of the Irish members to control all matters of a political or industrial nature, which solely affected the Irish membership to be in the control of an Irish committee or conference'.

I also wish to quote from *Eagle or Cuckoo? The Story of the* ATGWU *in Ireland* by Matt Merrigan, the Republic of Ireland District Secretary of the ATGWU at that time. Chapter 15, 'Unity at Last', deals with the decision on the proposed new constitution for uniting the Irish trade union movement (then divided into the Irish Trade Union Congress and the Congress of Irish Unions). The ITUC conference was held on 10 February 1959. The new constitution was moved by the President, Walter Carpenter:

> Larkin, winding up the debate, rounded on those who opposed the draft Constitution in trenchant terms: 'In 1953, after long and tortuous series of negotiations, we went on record with this statement: That this Conference should have in view the objective that the Irish Trade Union Movement should be wholly Irish based and Irish controlled. That was embodied in our Annual Report and every one of the unions whose representatives spoke today endorsed and accepted that principle! Are we to go back on it? We now have a draft Constitution carried out on that basis. First that it shall be Irish based and controlled. Second, that it shall apply to the whole of Ireland. Third, that there shall be no breaks in the links with our brothers across the channel. Isn't that what you sent us to get? Why then

would you repudiate the instructions you gave us? Tell us in particular where we have done violence to these instructions given by our affiliated unions? It would be fair to say of some that they are now being presented with unity which they never expected to be realized. There are objections as there would be to any Constitution of a Congress. But what we should be concerned with is whether it meets the instructions given ... I believe that Irish unions should be Irish based and controlled and make no apologies for it ... It appears today that some executives want us to protect them from their Irish membership ...'

The draft Constitution was adopted by 148 votes to 81. The CIU also adopted the draft Constitution and the ICTU was born ...

Some of the more right-wing elements of the British Labour movement were opposed to these particular clauses, believing that they would undermine the power of their general secretaries or executives in Britain. Andy Holmes dealt with their attitude in his speech, speaking on behalf of the General Executive Council of the T&G and its regional committees: 'The Amalgamated Transport Union is not afraid to trust the Irish membership to deal with all political and industrial matters, which affect the Irish membership; the Amalgamated Transport fully supports the new constitution of the ICTU ...' It would appear that the current leadership of the union just do not understand this situation. Had they understood this, they would have allowed the Irish region to investigate, if not all of these matters, then at the very least all of the matters, which have a political or industrial implication to them. The question must be asked: why is the General Secretary afraid to trust the Irish members? We are a collective movement and any of our faults should in the first place be examined by the committees that we serve: that is the normal position of most trade unionists. But there is an extra dimension: Ireland is a country, and there are laws which explicitly require the decisions of this nature to be made by elected bodies in Ireland.

At the biennial delegate conference earlier this year, Brother Eddie Cronin, who was a delegate from the Irish region, expressed a view to Bill Morris that he had made no allowance for the uniqueness of the Irish region. Bill Morris dismissed his comments by suggesting that there was no difference between Ireland and any other region. This is perhaps at the kernel of this dispute. There has historically always been an allowance for a different approach to be taken in Ireland, as the minutes of the Executive Council and the Irish regional committee will show, when full-time officers required the sanction of the General Executive Council to sit in a representative capacity on public bodies. Brother Norman Kennedy, the Regional Secretary in Ireland, was nominated to the old Northern Ireland Senate in Stormont.

The General Executive Council expressed their disapproval and he was requested not to take his seat. Norman Kennedy consulted with the regional committee and they backed his view. He retained his seat in the Senate and the executive minutes show that this matter was described as an embarrassment. Both the Irish regional committee and secretary won the day. A similar situation happened when the General Secretary of the Labour Party, Mr Brendan Halligan, complained to Jack Jones, the then General Secretary, that the Republic of Ireland District Secretary had threatened to disaffiliate the union from the Irish Labour Party. Jack Jones informed him that it was strictly a matter for the Irish membership.

The General Secretary has failed to understand the situation in Ireland. He has destroyed the reputation of the union in Ireland. He has removed me from the executive of the ICTU, which is contrary to the decisions of the Irish regional committee, which elected me to it, and for which he has no authority. This is contrary to Irish law, namely, the 1975 Trade Union Act. He has banned my participation in the civic forum, which is a chamber of civic groups in Northern Ireland set up to advise the new assembly, he has banned me from participating in the Northern Ireland Committee of the ICTU, he has banned me from speaking at the Desmond Greaves Summer School even though I was speaking there in a personal capacity. He does all this in the name of protecting my rights and protecting the union. The effect of these actions, however, undermines my rights both as a member and an employee, and destroys the reputation of the union.

The Amalgamated Transport and General Workers' Union is part of the Irish Labour movement and has made a unique contribution to the culture of Irish trade unionism over the years. From the foundation of the union in 1922 until my appointment, it is a fact that I am the first person to do the job of Regional Secretary who comes from a perceived Catholic and republican tradition and who has spent most of his life in the capital of Ireland. Given the complex situation in the North of Ireland regarding sectarianism, the civil strife and the war which has been waged for almost thirty years, the union had a responsibility, knowing the difficult situation that I was faced with in respect of my cultural background, to be supportive of me.

The union certainly had a duty of care in respect of both Brother McGlone and myself. A good number of the charges spread over almost a four-year period, and some precede my appointment as Regional Secretary. At no stage was there any counselling or assistance offered by the union to me. What we have here is the accumulation of trivial points which are stitched together after a period of years to attempt to justify the actions of the General Secretary. The General Secretary himself clearly states this in his letter of 5 December 2000 to me: 'Each complaint in itself would not necessarily give cause for concern, however when taken together there is a clear pattern relating to both the issues and the individuals involved.' This shows that the General Secretary allowed these issues to accumulate without discussing these matters in the region, informing us of any problems or affording any assistance in respect of any of the issues. The procedures in terms of warnings and counselling which were imposed but not accepted on 31 March 2001, were not even applied.

In the letter of suspension of 26 June 2001, no reason for suspension was given, yet the General Secretary states in the letter that he had evidence before him to warrant his actions. Why was this evidence not made available, and no reason given for it not being available? If he had this evidence, he had a duty to inform me of its contents prior to the suspension. The fact that he did not do so was negligent on his part. On the morning of the suspensions I returned from holidays, I travelled to Belfast from Dublin, I had made arrangements with Brother Ray Collins to discuss the train drivers' dispute, constitutional committees and a number of other matters. I arranged for the two executive members, the Republic of Ireland District Secretary and Regional Organizer, as well as the chairman of the regional committee to be in attendance. With hindsight, now it appears that this meeting and the arrangements surrounding it were just a piece of camouflage to allow Brother Ray Collins to deliver the General Secretary's letter and to summarily order me from my office and instruct me not to contact any of the officers or staff or any third parties with which the union engages. There were also damaging leaks to the press in the form of the *Irish Times* article, which attempted to smear me, together with radio programmes and other news items. During the week that followed a senior officer of the union, Brother Ben Kearney, made comment on the case from the ICTU conference on the main RTÉ news. This was grossly unfair to me as I was banned from speaking to the press and defending my good name. I did not receive the bundle of documents until approximately four weeks after the suspension. I received these on a Monday morning; however, these documents got extensive coverage in the London-based *Sunday Times* the previous day.

Regarding our train driver membership in the Republic, this was not dealt with or referred to in the investigation, which was reported to the Executive Council. No investigation into these matters was authorized by the General Executive Council, no interviews took place with any members in Region 3 regarding these allegations. Why was the region not informed that an investigation into these matters was to take place? Why was nobody interviewed? Who carried out this investigation? When was it concluded? Who, if anybody, made complaints in respect of the train driver membership? In regard to the jumble of allegations made regarding our train driver membership, I will deal with that later if necessary.

At this point I wish to reiterate that it is pointless to go any further due to the process and procedures involved. However, if this is not accepted I will proceed to deal with the specific allegations. …

Summary

Now I propose to recap some key points:

1. Legitimacy of procedures

I do not consider that this investigation has been conducted according to the principles of natural justice. I challenge both the legitimacy of the procedures adopted and their operation on the following grounds:

a) The procedures have not been agreed by the Officers' Committee, which negotiates on behalf of officers as employees of the union, but have been imposed by the General Secretary.

b) During the first month of my so-called 'precautionary' suspension, I was given no reasons at all for this action being taken against me, even though the letter of suspension dated 26 June 2001 from the person hearing this case, the General Secretary, stated that he possessed evidence justifying the suspension. Thus, either I was deliberately denied knowledge of the charges against me for a whole month, or the General Secretary did not possess the relevant evidence on the date he suspended me, and in stating that he did possess the evidence, was prejudging the case.

c) The security, neutrality and integrity of the entire investigation process have been seriously defective, and in such ways that the defects must have originated or been authorized at the highest level of the union. I cite two examples in particular:

During last summer's ICTU conference, while I was prohibited from having any contact with the media, Ben Kearney, a senior officer of the union in Dublin, who must have been acting with the authority of the General Secretary (as he is still in post and subject to no disciplinary action himself), commented on the case in terms detrimental and prejudicial to me on the main RTÉ news.

The day before I finally received the documents giving details of the case against me – and while I was still in complete ignorance of any charges

– there was extensive coverage of the details of the case in the London-based *Sunday Times*. If this was not a deliberate 'leak' sanctioned or orchestrated from Central Office, it was appalling negligence. In addition, *The Irish Times* carried a stream of stories damaging to me, in particular, in relation to implications of financial impropriety, in the month before I received documents from Central Office. Since they clearly did not come from me or anyone supporting me, and there is no reason to believe *The Irish Times* would actually concoct such stories, it is hard to escape the conclusion that they must have been 'leaked' or sanctioned by Central Office.

d) The person hearing this case, the General Secretary Bill Morris, the person who conducted the investigation, the Deputy General Secretary Margaret Prosser, and one of the key witnesses, the Assistant General Secretary Ray Collins, all came to the issue with a pre-existing hostility and prejudice towards me.

This hostility was reported by the Region 5 Regional Secretary to two former General Executive Council members, who were told that their seats would be under threat if they voted for me to be appointed as Regional Secretary (see letter from Brother Ray Sherlock dated 13 August 2001). Furthermore, in reply to questions at the first hearing, Margaret Prosser did not deny the accuracy of the way her position was characterized.

e) The person hearing this case, the General Secretary, had already made a prejudgement when in his letter of 5 December 2000 to Margaret Prosser, the Deputy General Secretary and the officer charged with carrying out the investigation, he said of the complaints made, that 'when taken together there is a clear pattern relating to both the issues and the individuals involved'. The question of whether there is 'a clear pattern' only arises once the investigation and these hearings are complete, and the quality of the complaints and the supporting evidence can be evaluated – indeed, that is the purpose of the entire process.

f) The person carrying out the investigation, Margaret Prosser, had her neutrality compromised by the above comment contained in her letter of instruction.

g) The report then drafted by Margaret Prosser, which is being relied upon in this hearing, was compiled without any formal interview with myself, and is therefore defective in its very origins.

h) Furthermore, the failure to accord me a formal interview, and the attendant failure to enable me to sign off on the interview notes as a true record (or to append my own reservations), places me in a worse position than all the other officers and staff in the union who Margaret Prosser chose to interview.

i) This failure to hold any interview is compounded by the completely inaccurate claim in Margaret Prosser's report that I was interviewed. In fact what happened were three informal conversations – in a hotel lounge, the Belfast union office, and in my car on the way from Belfast to Dublin. There was no formality or procedure adopted, no list of questions, and most crucially, no contemporaneous note taking. Indeed, if any notes were made after the event, I have never had sight of them, and have no knowledge of their existence.

j) Yet, in spite of the failure to interview me, in her report Margaret Prosser makes specific allegations relating to my state of mind. She says: 'The current Regional Secretary takes a lackadaisical view of his administrative and managerial duties to the point of carelessness and disinterest.' A 'lackadaisical view', 'carelessness', 'disinterest' are all terms relating to my consciousness. I challenge the admissibility of any such comments which are not related to information collected by direct interview with myself.

Finally, it is an essential principle of natural justice that charges against a person must be clear and specific. This has been far from the case in this procedure. Indeed, in replying to the individual charge sheet, I have frequently had to guess at the nature of the charge, and actually had to construct some charges myself so that I could give a reply.

2. Breach of legislation and ICTU rules

I further challenge the entire process in that it is in breach of

a) the law of the Republic of Ireland (1975 Trade Union Act), and
b) the constitution of the Irish Congress of Trade Unions

These require the Irish members of British-based unions, via their governing committee or their conference, to have control of political and industrial matters which solely affect the Irish membership. Most of the issues raised in the investigation and report fall within that definition.

Pursuant to the authority conferred by Irish law and the constitution of ICTU, on 15 December 2000 the Irish regional committee requested that it be allowed to investigate the various complaints at issue. This request was denied. Thus, not only have the Irish membership been denied the control required by the union's own rules, by domestic Irish law, and by the governing inter-union rules in Ireland, they have been actively excluded from any possible involvement at all.

At the same time, there has been direct contact behind the scenes with the institutions of Irish trade unionism by Central Office. There has been much speculation and rumour about meetings and discussions between senior British union personnel and senior people from the ICTU and SIPTU. In the nature of things, it is very hard to prove the degree of such contact. However, we do know for certain that Ray Collins, the Assistant General Secretary, had a meeting with Peter Cassells, the former General Secretary of ICTU.

This meeting was held without any prior discussion with myself as Regional Secretary or the regional committee, and its contents have never been reported to myself or the Committee. Thus, active exclusion of Irish involvement has been matched by at least one piece of active interference from Central Office over the heads of the Irish membership and its legitimate constitutional representatives.

3. Political discrimination

I further challenge the whole process for its inherent and fundamental political discrimination, both against the Irish membership of the union and against myself. This has the following aspects:

a) Loss of representation by Irish membership: During the period that I have been suspended, the Irish membership has not only been denied my direct industrial services, it has also lost my political/industrial representation in the following arenas:

The ICTU – where I was prevented from standing for election, notwithstanding the fact that I was nominated to the Executive of ICTU by the Irish Regional Committee of the union. This resulted in the union having no representation on the highest body of the Irish trade union movement for the first time since the foundation of the ICTU in 1959.

The Northern Ireland Committee of ICTU – although I am still a member, I have been forbidden attendance since 26 June 2001.

The Northern Ireland Civic Forum – a crucial advisory body to the Northern Ireland Assembly, whose meetings I have been forbidden to attend.

b) Interference in my political right to engage in debate and free speech: The General Secretary, who is hearing this case, has infringed my own political rights to engage in democratic political debate and interaction. He did this

by banning me from speaking at one of the longest established and most highly respected political forums in Ireland, the Desmond Greaves Summer School – even though I had been invited, and would have spoken, in my personal capacity – and

by preventing me – an Irish trade unionist and an Irish citizen – from participating in the ICTU Executive Committee, its Northern Ireland Committee and the Northern Ireland Civic Forum.

c) Rejection of Irish industrial relations institutions: There has been a total refusal to engage formally with established Irish industrial relations institutions. The

Labour Relations Commission, the Rights Commissioner Service, and, indeed, the Irish Congress of Trade Unions, have all sought to provide assistance – and all have been sent away. This is a political rejection of the governing industrial relations institutions in that part of Ireland where over one-third of the membership reside.

d) Discrimination on the grounds of politics, religious or cultural identity: In her report, the Deputy General Secretary, Margaret Prosser, castigates my predecessor as Irish Regional Secretary, John Freeman. Her description, if accurate, would mean that John Freeman, had, to all intents and purposes, put a knife to the heart of trade union principles of democracy, accountability and lay authority within the ATGWU. She describes him as 'a man of autocratic style and tight control', and of his time in office, she says:

> The lack of a Committee structure, the presence of full-time officers at the Irish BDC and as Branch Secretaries (pay roll vote?), have combined to undermine the independence and voice of the lay membership. A system of favouritism by the Regional Secretary towards certain lay members and paid officers, which resulted in being supported for positions, has left many activists and officers with a lack of confidence regarding their own power and influence.

As John Freeman's successor, I wish to emphasize that I regard all of this as appalling and unsubstantiated slurs on someone who has no opportunity to defend himself. However, from the point of view of a commitment to equality of treatment and a rejection of discrimination on religious, political or cultural identity grounds, once the Deputy General Secretary has made these criticisms, some crucial questions then arise.

Thus, how did my predecessor – whose alleged failings, if true, would constitute a comprehensively corrupt betrayal of the union and its Irish members – escape any investigation, report writing, 'precautionary' suspension, prohibition on political and industrial representational activity, disciplinary proceedings or even the most minor telling-off?

John Freeman was Regional Secretary for twenty-five years. The last seven of those years overlapped with the first seven years of the current General Secretary, Bill Morris's tenure. What qualities or attributes did this man of such alleged deficiencies possess that allowed him to escape any censure at all while he was in office?

To anyone who knows anything about Irish politics and history – and any General Secretary who presumes, as Bill Morris has done, to substitute his own authority and expertise for that of the members and elected representatives of this

Region, must presumably claim some degree of knowledge – there is one glaring distinction between myself and my predecessor. Indeed, it is what distinguishes me from all my predecessors.

In the union's entire history, I am the only Irish Regional Secretary to have been born and reared in the Republic of Ireland, the only one to come from the perceived Catholic and republican tradition, and the only one to identify culturally as a Catholic. I am also the only Irish Regional Secretary ever to have been subjected to any disciplinary proceedings at all.

Under the Fair Employment Act, once distinctions in 'personal political, cultural and religious characteristics', and in 'being the recipient of adverse treatment' have been identified, it is up to the person responsible for the adverse treatment to demonstrate fairness and equality in the application of such treatment. I challenge the General Secretary to fulfil this obligation.

4. Industrial Relations Practice

I further challenge the entire process in that, in its treatment of me as an employee, the process breaches all good standards of industrial relations practice. This has the following aspects:

a) As noted earlier, the procedures being employed have not been agreed with the Officers' Committee but rather have been unilaterally imposed by the General Secretary, Bill Morris.

b) As noted earlier, I was not treated equally with other officers and staff in that I was never formally interviewed during the investigation carried out by the Assistant General Secretary, Margaret Prosser.

c) The General Secretary moved straight to disciplinary proceedings, rather than giving me the opportunity, as would be the case in properly conducted industrial affairs, to comment on the report of the investigation.

d) It is normal practice that where concerns are felt about an employee's behaviour or performance, there is preliminary discussion, perhaps counselling, and even, if necessary, a verbal warning, in order to try to improve matters and avert any need for more severe disciplinary action. In particular, a good and responsible employer puts in considerable effort to assisting a long-standing employee who is falling short of the mark but has a hitherto unblemished record. Even more so this is the case where the employee is in any respects a 'trailblazer' – the first black person to hold a senior position, or the first woman, the first gay person – or the first Southern Irish Catholic, who is taking over in a place that is only just emerging from a thirty-year period of war.

I have been an active member of the union for thirty-nine years and a paid officer for twenty-three years. During my entire 23-year service until the events leading up to this hearing, there has never once been a complaint about me from a member or from a constitutional committee. As these hearings have made absolutely clear, no evidence has been produced during the Deputy General Secretary's investigation, or at these hearings, which suggests that I have fallen short in any way that justifies any level of formal disciplinary action.

However, assuming for the sake of argument that genuine concerns have been felt about my behaviour or performance, what is remarkable is that no preliminary discussion, counselling or any other support or problem-solving strategies whatsoever have been adopted. Instead, there has been a direct move to the most public and serious level of disciplinary action.

Final comments

I have spent a great deal of time since June of this year trying to work out why these actions have been taken against me, especially as they are reliant on such wretchedly thin material, which hardly qualifies in any way for the description 'evidence'. I have also been baffled as to the reasons for the adoption of such extremely deficient procedures. I am forced to two conclusions:

a) 'No different from Finchley': The former British Prime Minister, Margaret Thatcher, once famously said that Northern Ireland was as British as Finchley. Ignoring the history of our union (which I detailed in my opening statement at the first hearing), the General Secretary, Bill Morris, told Brother Eddie Cronin, a delegate from the Irish region to the BDC, that there was no difference between Ireland and any other Region.

As Irish Regional Secretary, and previously as District Secretary, District Organizer, regional committee member, shop steward and rank and file member, my loyalty to the ATGWU has always been total. And this loyalty has stood perfectly comfortably alongside my pride in my own nationality and assertion of Irish political independence. I believe either that:

Brother Morris genuinely does not understand how Irishness and ATGWU loyalty can go hand in hand – so long as the political independence of Ireland is respected. He therefore perceives a profound challenge and disloyalty in actions of mine and of this Region which carry no such intended threat, as a result of which perception he is convinced that I must be removed at all cost, or

Brother Morris is simply not prepared to accept that the Irish region, North and South, is politically quite different from all other Regions in the union, and is determined to remove me for consistently asserting and standing up for that difference.

b) Political Isolation: It is no secret that the stand I and the regional committee have taken on many issues is unpopular with the Irish government, and with many senior people in the trade union movement in the Republic (e.g. in ICTU and SIPTU). I can only speculate as to whether this has led the General Secretary into the misapprehension that I am largely isolated in the Irish trade union movement and can, consequently, be removed from office irrespective of the quality of evidence against me or the procedures adopted to carry out the removal.

If this is the case, then I would like the General Secretary to think again. Although trade union leaders and Prime Ministers may not like my views, there is a great deal of evidence that ordinary union members (both in our union, and in the wider movement in Ireland) are very comfortable with them. Indeed, if the General Secretary pushes matters to the ultimate stage of dismissal, he will find himself a pariah among the regional committee, other constitutional committees of the union in Ireland and the ATGWU membership generally.

The future

During the last few months I consider that I have been treated in an extremely unfair and hurtful manner, that I have suffered serious and unlawful discrimination, that my national and cultural identity have been treated with contempt, and that every effort has been made to publicly humiliate me and destroy my reputation. Nevertheless, my commitment to the ATGWU and its membership remains total.

The measure of this commitment is as follows. If these proceedings are called to a halt and I am restored to my position as Regional Secretary, I give an unconditional guarantee that I will take no legal action against the union. In particular, I will not pursue the many examples of seriously discriminatory action contrary to the Fair Employment legislation that have been taken against me.

I will put all that has happened behind me. I will work with the General Secretary and everyone else involved to heal the wounds that have been caused, and to rebuild the confidence, morale and standing of the ATGWU throughout the island of Ireland.

Thank you for your attention.

Index

Adams, Gerry 64, 163

Adams, Jack 133, 155

Aer Lingus 124–7

Aer Rianta 127

Agnew, Paddy 97

Ahern, Bertie 126, 143

Aiken, Frank 70–1, 102

Aiken, John 155

Alberanti (manager at Fiat) 59, 65

Allen, Woody 118

Amalgamated Engineering Union 65

Amicus 160, 164

Anglo Irish Bank 161–2

Armstrong's 74, 127

Association of Scientific, Technical and
    Managerial Staffs 46–7

ATGWU (Amalgamated Transport
    and General Workers' Union) xv,
    30, 54, 66–8, 94, 139, 143–7, 150, 159,
    178–9 *see also* O'Reilly, Mick
        Dundalk 88–91, 95, 97, 100, 112

Automotive General Engineering and
    Mechanical Operatives' Union 125

Bakers' Union 4, 42

Ballyfermot 2–3, 44, 63

Barr, Andy 61, 82–3, 122–3

Barry, Tom 78

Beatles 42

Begg, David xv

Behan, Brendan 33

Behan, Dominic 20

Behan, John 126, 162

Bell, Michael 109

Benn, Tony 62–3, 107

Berlinguer, Enrico 79

Bernstein, Eduard 48

Bevin, Ernie 66–7

Bewley, Victor 40

Blair, Tony 19, 62, 129

Boland, Kevin 41

Bourne, Harry 20, 24

Boyd, Andy 85

Boyle, Hilary 37

Branigan, Desmond 21

Brecht, Bertolt 6

Bree, Declan 174

Brezhnev, Leonid 48, 81–2

British and Irish Communist
    Organization 37

Brittain 60, 73–4

Brown, Gordon 129

Browne, Bernard 10, 18–19, 26, 28, 35,
    38, 40, 145, 154, 165, 174

Browne, Danny 56

Browne, Noël 110

Bruton, John 92, 129

Burke, Ray 126

Byrne, Noel 107

Cairns, Norman xvi, 149

Camfield, Barry 155

Campbell, Johnny 36

Carmody, Paddy 9, 21, 28–31, 34, 46, 52, 62, 79, 85, 90

Carpenter, Walter 177

Carroll's 94–5

Carson, Joanna 146

Casement, Roger 60

Cashman, Tom 156

Cassells, Peter 144, 184

Catholic Church xvii, 4–5, 12, 43, 77, 84

Catholic Workers' College 16, 58

China 47, 70–1, 84

Chrysler 75

Churchill, Winston 60, 67

Citizen Army 25

CIU (Congress of Irish Unions) 177–8

Claffey, Úna 108

Clann na Poblachta 4

Cluskey, Peter xv, 150

Coates, Ken 35

Collins, Ray xvi–xvii, 122, 145, 176, 180, 182, 184

Comintern 28–9, 47

Communist Party (CP) 14–15, 19–24, 42, 52, 61, 63–4, 89, 109 see also Irish Workers' Party
    in Czechoslovakia 46, 50
    Historians Group 21–2
    in Italy 59

Communist Party of Ireland (CPI) 77–8, 84, 132, 163

Communist Party of Northern Ireland (CPNI) 28, 46, 64, 67, 78

Condit, Bill 147, 154, 176

Confederation of Irish Industry 73

Connolly, James 12, 16, 25, 29, 64, 96, 98, 109

Connolly, Roddy 77, 163

Connolly Association 19, 61

Connolly Youth Movement (CYM) 33–6, 46 see also O'Reilly, Mick

Conroy, John 69

Cork Operative Butchers' Society 145

Cork Socialist Party 78

Cork Street, Dublin 1

Cornish, Valerie xvii, 137

Cosgrave, Liam 39

Cosgrove, Frank 103–6

Costello, Séamus 40

Coughlan, Tony 63, 72, 76

Cowen, Brian 166

Crea, Mickey 58

Criminal Assets Bureau 161

Cronin, Anthony 85

Cronin, Eddie 178, 187

Cuba 82

Cunningham, Billy 13

Czechoslovakia 46–7, 49–50, 79–80, 82–4, 119

Daily Worker 19, 32

Davison, Madge 32

de Búrca, Máirín 40, 63

De La Salle school, Ballyfermot 6

de Valera, Éamon 13, 38, 42, 70–1, 74

de Valera, Vivion 70

Deakin, Arthur 66

Deasy, Joe 33, 84

Deery, Lillian xvi

Dennehy, Dennis 39–40
Dent, Tom 10
Desmond, Barry 75, 107–9
Desmond Greaves School 32, 64,
    150–1, 179, 184
Devlin, Bernadette 97, 123
Devlin, Paddy 85
Devves, Jim 9–10
Dickens, Charles 127, 153
Dimitrov, Georgi 148–9
Doherty, Pat 162
Douglas, Charlie 121–3
Dromey, Jack 129–30
Dublin Council of Trade Unions 41,
    46, 72
Dublin Housing Action Committee
    (DHAC) 37–42, 55–6, 63
Duff, Thomas 174
Dundalk 89–91 see also ATGWU
Dunne, Seán 38, 40, 56

Early, Packie 33, 84
Ebbs, Billy 28
Echo 94, 96, 98, 154
Edwards, Mrs Frank 174
Edwards, Sean 174
EEC (European Economic
    Community) 70–4, 89, 155
Ellenberg, Marty 91–2
Elsby, Jimmy xvi, 147, 157–8
Ennis, John 175–6
ESB (Electricity Supply Board) 54, 75
ESB Officers' Assocation 117
ETU (Electrical Trades Union) 23, 28
EU (European Union) 72

Fabian Society 25
Farrell, Michael 32
Faulkner, William 54
Federated Union of Employers 73
Fianna Fáil 25, 42, 70–2, 93, 102, 120,
    126, 168
Fiat 55–60, 93, see also O'Reilly, Mick:
    employment
Fielding, Mark 125
Fine Gael 39, 72, 91, 106–7, 168–9
Finnegan, Paddy 125
FitzGerald, Eithne 109
FitzGerald, Garret 98–9, 106–7
Flanagan, Luke 'Ming' 163
Fleming, Eric 174
Fleming, Gerry 48
Flynn, Phil 107, 149, 161–2
Fogarty report 117
Fóir Teoranta 92
Freeman, John 97, 121–4, 131–3, 135,
    139, 141, 146–7, 159, 185
Friends of Sinn Féin 139

Galbraith, Bertie 74
Gannon, Jack 72
Garland, Seán 62
Geehan, Tommy 67
General Electric Company, Coventry 18
General Motors (GM) 127–9
Georgia 80
Geraghty, Des 144, 148
Geraghty, Séamus 41, 122
Gide, André 14
Gladstone, William 62
Goldberg, Gerald 78
Goodman, Larry 100–2

Goold, Neil 80–1
Gorbachev, Mikhail 118–19
Goulding, Cathal 40, 56
Graham, Seán 157
Gramsci, Antonio 12, 20, 125
Greaves, Desmond 61, 63–4, 149 see
    also Desmond Greaves School
Gregory, Tony 162–3
Griffiths, George 57–8
Grossmann, Vasily 5
Grove Turkeys 102–6
Guthrie, Woody 54

Halligan, Brendan 109, 124, 179
Halpin, Kevin 132
Hanly, David 143
Harland & Wolff 30, 137
Harney, Mary 128
Harp brewery 90, 93
Harris, Eoghan 63
Harris, Noel 46–7, 83
Haughey, Charles 75, 93, 98–9, 106
Hayden, Patricia 33
Heath, Edward 71
Hendy, John 156
Hendy report 156
Higgins, Eddie 22–3
Higgins, Joe 110, 134
Higgins, Michael D. 107, 120
Hitler, Adolf 148–9
Hobsbawm, Eric 22, 82, 118
Hodgers, Brendan 98–9, 151, 154, 158
Hodgers, Sheila 98
Holmes, Andy 30, 69, 177
Holmes, Mick 56–7
Horner, Arthur 66

Howard's 8–9
Hull, Billy 122
Hungary 28, 50, 83
Hunt, Jim 175
Hyde, Douglas 14

Ian, Janis 43
Iarnród Éireann 143–4
Ibárurri, Dolores ('La Pasionaria') 49
IBEC (Irish Business and Employers'
    Confederation) 149
ICTU (Irish Congress of Trade Unions)
    see also O'Reilly, Mick xv, 68–9, 73,
    93–5, 97–8, 123, 126, 129, 147–8, 159,
    166, 177–9, 183–5, 188
IDATU (Irish Distributive and
    Administrative Trade Union) 103
ILDA (Irish Locomotive Drivers'
    Association) 143–5, 147
Institute for Workers' Control 35
IRA (Irish Republican Army) 40, 56,
    77 *see also* Provisional IRA
Ireland-USSR Society 31
Irish Marxist Society 85
Irish Parliamentary Party 168
Irish Productivity Centre 92
Irish Socialist 9, 14–15, 30–1, 46, 49 *see*
    also O'Reilly, Mick
Irish Workers' League 78
Irish Workers' Party (IWP) 14–16,
    19, 25, 27–8, 37, 39, 62, 78 *see also*
    O'Reilly, Mick
IRSP (Irish Republican Socialist
    Party) 136
ISME (Irish Small and Medium
    Enterprises Association) 125

ITGWU (Irish Transport and General Workers' Union) 9, 16, 19, 41, 66, 89–90, 94–5, 100

ITUC (Irish Trade Union Congress) 177

Jeffares, George 31, 46, 108

Jeffares, Marion 31

Johnston, Roy 63, 84

Jones, Jack 93, 122, 124, 179

Kautsky, Karl 48

Kavanagh, Robbie 9

Kay Security 56

Kearney, Ben xv–xvi, 180–1

Keating, Justin 15, 72–4, 86

Keating, Michael 125–6

Kelly, Jimmy xvi, 148–50, 165

Kennedy, Norman 66–9, 131, 178–9

Kenny report 37, 41–2

Kent, Fr Edmund 58

Kerrigan, Gene 151

Khrushchev, Nikita 34

Klugman, James 21, 29, 36, 154

Koestler, Arthur 14

Kyle, Sam 131

La Pasionaria (Dolores Ibárurri) 49

Labour Court 58, 117, 128, 149, 162

Labour Left 106–9, 120, 123

Labour Party 15–16, 37, 42, 72–3, 75, 78, 85, 106–10, 120, 162, 166, 168–9, 179
    British 19, 24–5, 61, 78
    Northern Ireland 64

Lambe, Noel 17

Larkin, Jim 2, 47, 69, 94, 118, 177–8

Larkin, Jim, Jr 86

Larkin Jones, James (Jack) 66, 93, 122, 124, 179

Lehane, Con 30

Lemass, Seán 70–2

Lenihan, Brian 120, 166

Lenin, Vladimir 25, 51, 77, 163, 168

Leningrad 81

Lepp, Ignace 14

Lincoln & Nolan 10–11, 18

Lindberg, Walter 79

Liverpool 134–5

Livingstone, Ken 123

Longo, Luigi 79

Lynch, Gilbert 94

Lynch, John 92

McAleer, Peter 102

Macardle's 90

McBride, Harry xvi

McBrinn, Liam 131–5, 138–9, 176

McCann, Éamonn 11–12

McCarthy, Mick 67

McCluskey, Len 156

MacColl, Ewan 20

McCorry, Kevin 151–3

McCoy, Jackie xvi

McCrea, Willie 137

McCready, Albert 74–5, 145, 148

McCusker, Joe 147, 176

Mac Gabhann, Liam 25

Mac Giolla, Tomás 62, 72

McGlone, Eugene xi, xiii, xvi, 131, 131–3, 144–6, 149, 151, 153, 155, 179

McGowan, Paddy 14

MacGowran, Jack 26

McGuinness, Martin 64, 139
McKearn's Motors 74
McKenna, Siobhán 26
McKenna, Ted 60, 148
McLoone, Peter 144
McLaughlin, Mitchel 162
McLoughlin, Jimmy 103, 105
McMullen, William 94
McNulty, Phil 152, 156
Manufacturing Science and Finance
    Union 160
Marshall, Fiona 146, 176
Marshalsea House 37
Marx, Karl 2, 16, 51, 165, 168
May Roberts (chemist) 9, 11
Merrigan, Mattie 41, 66, 68, 75, 87–8,
    90, 93–6, 103, 106–7, 110, 121, 124,
    127, 129, 138, 146, 177
Mikoyan, Anastas 81
Militant 110
Mitchell, John 103–4
Monckton, Ivan 133–4
Montgomery, Johnny 33
Mooney, Johnny 33
Morning Star 19–20, 141
Morris, Bill xvii, 26, 69, 129–30, 133–5,
    138–41, 145–53, 155–7, 175–82, 185–8
Moy Park 134
Mullen, Mickey 41, 68, 94
Mulready, Liam 38, 98, 174
Mulvey, Kieran 149
Murphy, Con 96
Murphy, Dan 144
Murphy, Noel 150
Murray, Len 68, 123

National Union of Mineworkers 66
National Union of Sheet Metal
    Workers 125
NATO (North Atlantic Treaty
    Organisation) 70
NBRU (National Bus and Rail Union)
    133–4
Newe, John 152, 156
Nolan, Johnny 15, 30, 47–8, 80,
    163, 174
Nolan, Sam 28, 31, 33, 46–7, 52, 72,
    108, 168
Northern Ireland 51, 61–5, 69, 78, 84,
    116, 119–20, 122, 124, 136, 139, 146,
    151, 177–9, 187
Northern Ireland Civic Forum 179, 184
NUDL (National Union of Dock
    Labourers) 97
NUVB (National Union of Vehicle
    Builders) 11, 56, 59–60, 65–6, 97

O'Casey, Seán 16, 26
Ó Cionnaith, Seán 40
O'Connell, John 37
O'Connor, Jack 164
O'Donnell, Peadar 34
Ogle, Brendan 145
O'Grady (foreman) 17
O'Leary, Michael 40–1, 72, 106
O'Malley, Des 73
O'Neill, Hughie 57–9
O'Neill, Paddy 23
O'Reilly, Emma 99
O'Reilly, Frank 125
O'Reilly, John 56–8, 60
O'Reilly, Louise 44, 99

O'Reilly, Mary xvii, 42–4, 99, 148

O'Reilly, Mick

    and ATGWU: 87–93, 100, 106, 162; leaves 165; regional secretary 123–4, 134–41, 142 (campaign 131–3); suspension xi–xiii, xvi–xviii, 145–58 (hearing 152–4, 175–88; reinstatement 151, 156)

    and bank workers 161–2

    in Belfast 135–8, 156–7

    and the CP 14–15, 19, 28, 34, 42, 45, 119, 169

    and the CPI 78–9, 83–6, 108

    and the CYM 33–4, 46, 53, 79, 173–4

    daughters 44, 99

    and DHAC 37–42, 63

    and Desmond Greaves School 32, 64, 150–1, 179, 184

    early life 1–7

    early trade union involvement 10–12

    education: 6–7, 16–17; return to 167

    employment: early jobs 8–17; Fiat 55–60, 93 (shop steward 57–60, 74); temporary 53–4

    and employment appeals tribunal 167

    in England 18–26

    and ESB 116–17

    father 1–4, 19

    and feminism 32

    and Fine Gael 107

    first Communion 4–5

    and ICTU: 123, 143–4; runs for vice presidency 163–4

    ill-health 6, 60

    and industrial action 22–3, 56–8, 73–5, 103–5

    and Irish Marxist Society 85

    and *Irish Socialist* 30, 49, 53

    and Irish Workers' Party 19, 32–3, 53

    and ITGWU 94–5

    and Labour Left 106–9, 123

    and the Labour Party 15, 85, 106–10

    management style 164–5

    marriage 43

    and the media 141, 142–3

    mother 2–5, 19

    negotiating: 91–2, 100–1; style 21

    political awakening 14–16

    and racism 24

    reading 55

    reputation xi–xiii

    and Sinn Féin 162–3

    and SIPTU 167

    sisters 3, 5–6, 9, 19

    and Trades Council 167–8

    unemployment 42–3, 53–5

    views: capitalism 119; civil rights movement 61–2; collective bargaining 73, 112–14, 116; communism 118, 169; Cuba 82; democratic centralism 50–1; economic crash 165–6; EEC/EU 70–4, 76; eighth amendment 98–9; euro 76; Fine Gael 92; ICTU 118; Labour Party 110; Marxism 168–9; national wage agreements 112–14, 166; negotiating 112–13; neutrality 167; Nice treaty 143; Northern

Ireland 62–5, 78; republicanism 98, 151; running unions 93; sectarianism 95, 109, 136–8; self-determination 48–9; social partnership 116; socialism 166; Soviet Union 82–4, 118–19; strike-breaking 104; strikes 51, 73, 75–6, 106; unions 11–12, 51, 114, 117–18, 143, 159–61, 167, 169 visits: Georgia 80; Soviet Union 79–81

O'Reilly, Suzanne 44, 99

O'Reilly, Tommy 125

O'Riordan, Manus 34

O'Riordan, Michael (Mick) 25, 27–31, 33, 35, 38, 40, 46–7, 49–52, 54, 78, 81–4, 132, 150, 155

O'Rourke, Lillie 46

O'Rourke, Mary 144

O'Rourke, Seán 46

Orwell, George 14

O'Sullivan, Turlough 149

O'Toole, Joe 144, 147

O'Toole, Peter 26

Packard 75, 127–9, 145

Palme Dutte, Rajani 29, 36

People's College 16

Pinochet, Augusto 128

Pollitt, Harry 15, 23

Powell, Enoch 24

Powell, Paddy 19

Prague 46 see also Czechoslovakia

Progressive Democrats 90

Prosser, Margaret 133, 145–6, 152, 155, 175–6, 182–3, 185–6

Provisional IRA (Provos) 62, 64–5, 97, 104–5

Rabbitte, Pat 108, 128

Rainier, Peter 152

Revell, Brendan 92

Revolutionary Workers' Groups 67, 77

Reynolds, Albert 102

Roberts, Ruaidhrí 72

Robinson, Mary 120

Rogers, Bernard 174

Ronan, Jimmy 13

St Petersburg see Leningrad

S&S Corrugated 91

Sands, Bobby 97

Semperit 53, 73

Service Employees International Union 160

Shanahan, Jerry 164

Shaw, George Bernard 16, 159

Sheehy Skeffington, Owen 15

Shelepin, Alexander 83

Sherlock, Ray 175–6

Shorts 122–3

Sinclair, Betty 46–7, 61, 82

Sinn Féin 37, 39, 72, 139, 162–3, 168–9

SIPTU (Scientific, Industrial, Professional and Technical Union) 11, 125, 143–4, 164, 167, 183, 188

Sitting Bull 125

Socialist Labour Party (SLP) 110

Socialist Party 34

Socialist Workers' Party 150

Solzhenitsyn, Aleksandr 80

Soviet Union 4, 6, 21–2, 28–9, 34–5, 42, 46, 48–51, 79–84, 118–19, 127, 166, 168

Spellman, Cardinal 71

Spring, Dick 108–9

Stafford, Gerry 26

Stagg, Emmet 107

Stalin, Joseph 4, 31, 34, 77, 81, 148–9, 166

Stalker, John 156

Stepinac, Archbishop 70

Stern, Andy 160

Stirling's 9–10

Stuart, Dawn 155

Sweeney, Pat 75

Sweetman, Fr Michael 37, 40

Taylor, Mervyn 107, 128, 133

Team Aer Lingus 124–6, 149, 162

TEEU (Technical Engineering and Electrical Union) 117, 125

Telesis report 71, 83

TGWU (Transport and General Workers' Union) 11, 26, 30, 65–7, 69, 129–30, 131, 138–9, 142, 146–8, 150–8, 175, 178
    Officers' National Committee 151–2, 181

Thatcher, Margaret 114, 177, 198

Thompson, Alex xvi

Tinkler, Jimmy 106–7, 117

Tito, Josip 70

Togliatti, Palmiro 59

Tone, Wolfe 28–9, 34, 96 see also Wolfe Tone Society

Trade Unionists for Irish Unity and Independence 98, 123

Trades Council 89–90, 97, 167–8
    see also Dublin Council of Trade Unions

Trotsky, Leon 124, 168

TUC (Trades Union Congress) 61, 83, 123

Tunney, Hugh 100, 102

Tunney's 102, 105

Ulster Workers' Council 122–3

Unite (Unite the Union) 68, 160

USSR see Soviet Union

Vietnam 70, 84

Walsh, Éamonn 41

Walsh, Martin 145

Warwick University 19

Waters, Raymond 88

Wayne, Naomi 85

Wheatley, Billy 10, 12–13, 107

Whelan, Marty 143

Whitaker, T.K. 71

White, Alex 149

Whitty, Fergus 146

Wilson, Harold 19, 22, 61

Withers, Sharon xvi

Wolfe Tone Society 63

Woodley, Tony 155–6, 158

Workers' Union of Ireland 54, 100

Young, Tim 49

Young Communist League 35, 80